Table for One
New York City

The Solo Diner's Restaurant Guide

Michael Kaminer
with Jonathan Boorstein

Contemporary Books

*Chicago New York San Francisco Lisbon London Madrid Mexico City
Milan New Delhi San Juan Seoul Singapore Sydney Toronto*

Library of Congress Cataloging-in-Publication Data

Kaminer Michael.
   Table for one, New York City : the solo diner's restaurant
guide / Michael Kaminer, with Jonathan Boorstein.
      p.   cm.
   Includes index.
   ISBN 0-658-00697-5
   1. Restaurants—New York (State) —New York—
Guidebooks.   I. Boorstein, Jonathan.   II. Title.

TX907.3.N72 N448   2001
647.95747'1—dc21   2001028567

Contemporary Books

*A Division of The **McGraw-Hill** Companies*

1 2 3 4 5 6 7 8 9 0   AGM/AGM   0 9 8 7 6 5 4 3 2 1

ISBN 0-658-00697-5

This book was set in Adobe Garamond
Printed and bound by Arcata Martinsburg-Quebecor

Cover and series design by Rattray Design
Cover photograph copyright © Artville

McGraw-Hill books are available at special quantity discounts to use as
premiums and sales promotions, or for use in corporate training
programs. For more information, please write to the Director of Special
Sales, Professional Publishing, McGraw-Hill, Two Penn Plaza, New
York, NY 10121-2298. Or contact your local bookstore.

This book is printed on acid-free paper.

$Contents$

INTRODUCTION

THIS BOOK WAS borne of good and bad experiences dining solo in New York City and around the world. I've been fawned over in Madrid by a maternal waitress who spoke no English, shoved into a suffocating communal table at a packed vegetarian dive in Paris, served with a smile in Bombay by the most solicitous waiters I've ever met, ignored at a cheap snack spot in Hong Kong buzzing with business-people on lunch break, and treated like royalty at a hotel dining room in St. Petersburg (Russia, not Florida).

At home in New York, dining solo is an equally hit-or-miss proposition. In a city with an enormous number of single professionals and visitors, you'd think restaurants would welcome tables for one. But for every memorable meal I've experienced on my own, there's an infuriating experience I want to forget. With this book, I'm hoping to share some of those experiences to help make all of your solo meals a pleasure.

A little history: I've been dining out solo as long as I can remember, but really began appreciating the experience when I started my own business, back in 1992. After a twelve-hour day on the phone or talking to associates, the last thing I wanted after work was more talk. So I began blocking out dinner—to the extent I could—as private time.

It was, and still is, one of my most precious luxuries. It's pure pleasure to be able to visit a restaurant, choose my table, pace my meal, read, write, observe, savor, and contemplate.

We're lucky in New York. Along with old standbys like coffee shops and Chinese restaurants, we've got an abundance of places that serve full menus at the counter or bar and otherwise welcome and accommodate solo diners. Sometimes you can tell by looking; sometimes (bad) experience is the only litmus test.

After all these years, I've developed some survival skills for the times when the meal's not so pleasant. As I imagine a lot of you have, I found complaining very difficult my first few times out alone. The last thing I wanted was to call more attention to myself. But after another lousy table, or another episode of apathetic service, or yet another waiter rushing me so a couple could take my place, I learned the value of raising my voice.

I hope I can help closet solo diners, who wish they could confidently request a table for one but secretly have nightmares about the scenario. For so many people, the primary emotion a table for one inspires is fear—fear of what others will think, fear that a restaurant won't treat them with respect, fear they won't be able to fill a long stretch of mealtime on their own. By proving that a solo meal can be a pleasure, I hope to help overcome that.

Luckily, there seems to be more awareness than ever of solo diners as a legitimate consumer force. Maybe it's the ever-increasing number of business travelers, maybe the spiraling number of single professionals. In any case, the net result seems to be better treatment by dining establishments.

"When I sit down to eat alone," Pamela Margoshes wrote recently in the *Washington Post*, "I am completely relaxed and happy in my own company. What could be wrong with that?"

What indeed?

I'm hoping to share that happiness with you in this book, as well as offer some caveats and tips gleaned from years of being both appreciated and abused by waitstaff:

Assert yourself.

If you're given what's obviously a lousy table, don't accept it. Complaining makes some solo diners uncomfortable, because there's no one at your side to vouch for you. But nine times out of ten, my gripes have been validated (and apologized for) by a server or manager.

Sit near a window.

Nothing makes some solo diners more uncomfortable than being plopped at a two-top in the middle of a restaurant. A place by a window not only gives you choice seating on the periphery of the room, where you'll get the best view of the room, but also offers terrific people-watching opportunities if interest in your reading material wanes.

Pick a well-lighted spot.

Most solo diners I know love to read while they eat. You'll find it a lot more difficult if you have to squint at your newspaper through the gloom at a dimly lit corner table. If the lighting's abysmal, ask if it can be altered.

Avoid communal tables.

In theory, communal tables sound ideal. In reality, they usually recreate the dining ambience of an economy-class airplane flight.

Don't rush, and don't let them rush you.

Part of the pleasure of dining solo is the luxury of pacing yourself. Once, at a San Francisco restaurant-of-the-moment, a waitress noted that I'd been sitting over my lunch for ninety minutes. I was about to get defensive when she told me how much she admired my ability to take time for myself and truly enjoy my meal.

Solo-friendly service is not necessarily proportional to price.

This is New York in the twenty-first century. Paying a lot for anything doesn't guarantee a good experience. The same holds true, sadly, for restaurants. As I discovered in the course of researching this book, many of the most expensive and exalted places treat solo diners the same way they'd treat houseguests who'd overstayed their welcome. The point is, don't spend a lot of money on a meal just because you think it'll secure you special treatment. I've highlighted some of the better high-end places here to save you the trouble.

Make friends with servers and maitre d's, especially at places where you plan to return.

I can't count the number of times I've been given a table—for one—ahead of waiting hordes because I was friendly with a host, hostess, or server. You'll also find special requests and off-the-menu favors a lot easier to fulfill when waitstaff like you.

If a table's impossible, sit at the counter or bar.

Sometimes it is unreasonable to expect a table for one—strolling into a hot New York restaurant at nine on a Friday night, for example. But most respectable establishments will serve a full menu at the bar, which can offer a very pleasant alternative to a crowded room.

Solo-Dining
Survival Strategies

THEO IS ONE of the few people in New York who actually wants to be in food service. He is an out-of-work sous-chef, as opposed to, say, another out-of-work actor.

Like all of us, Theo has certain life occasions he likes to celebrate with a fancy meal. For birthdays and other special events, he calls up one or two of New York's top restaurants and makes a reservation for one.

Of course, not everyone has quite Theo's aplomb. For most of us, it takes a bit of luck and guesswork. One basic strategy is to arrive at an off hour—when the place is just opening, or after the main crush has left, but the kitchen is not yet closed.

A variation of Theo's idea works when you're from out of town. Most hotels have some sort of concierge service. Have the concierge make the reservation. There's a big difference between your calling up and saying, "I'm Joe Shmoe. I'd like a table for one for six P.M.," and the concierge calling up and saying, "Hi. I'm Tiffany. I'm the concierge at [your hotel]. We have a guest here who would like a reservation for tonight at six." The restaurant may or may not take your reservation. The restaurant will likely take one from the hotel. The restaurant wants the hotel to recommend the place and to call again.

By the way, don't call up yourself and lie, either about being Tiffany or about the number of guests there will be. The host or hostess heard about the table for two, one of whom cancelled at the last minute, long before you thought it up.

As for tables, I don't mind being seated at a table in the bar. I also don't mind being seated near the kitchen or near a waiter's station. I look upon that as a way to attract attention that might not otherwise come my way. I know of one solo diner who would rather be at a table that faces a wall than "to face someone I'm not talking to."

Solo dining usually involves something to read or something to write. The newspaper is traditional, but a book or a magazine would certainly do as well. Whichever you pick, make sure that there's enough left to read to last you through your meal. I find a stack of two or three magazines works best.

Writing in restaurants is so popular that David Mamet used it as the title of a book. And just about any sort of writing will do. My friends ask where I find time to write a couple of hundred postcards whenever I go away. The answer is: writing postcards at restaurants while I'm dining solo. My championship average is twenty cards per meal.

If fiction or correspondence isn't what you'd like to do, how about updating your planner? I can remember one waiter apologizing for interrupting my power lunch (for one) by bringing my order.

While playing with your FiloFax is OK, working with a notebook is not, even if you remember to turn off all the bells and whistles. For some reason, pen and paper is intriguing while technology is intrusive. A handheld digital assistant is probably all right, but if your gizmo beeps, you are no longer asserting your right to your own space as a solo diner, you are infringing upon the rights of others.

Also on the inadvisable list are beepers and cell phones. If you have to speak to someone during lunch, why didn't you ask that person to join you for lunch? And the table next to you won't be impressed with your importance. It will just be annoyed. Many people are convinced that whoever is calling them or interrupting them is much more important than what they're doing. Don't let yourself be interrupted at the table and don't interrupt others.

In addition to the suggestions we've already made, here are a few basic concepts to help you be a successful solo diner wherever you may go.

Know thyself.

It's all very well and good for me to tell you to assert yourself. I live in New York. I'm case-hardened. You have to know the stress levels at which you are still able to function and work within them. If you're shy, asking for a table for one at an off hour at a local restaurant is quite an accomplishment. Work your way up before you tackle single bookings at four-star restaurants.

Think strategically.

Think before you feed. As much as I hate to admit it, dining solo sometimes involves a trade-off. Don't try restaurants during their rush hours. Outwit them. Figure out when they'd love to see you. Look for off hours, like six to seven P.M. or ten to eleven P.M. Clues they want your business might be early-bird or pretheater specials. Prix fixe is also a subtle hint that a place is looking.

Take a chance.

Try a brand new place no one has reviewed yet—or a cuisine you've never heard of. Often, these restaurants are trying to build business and will see you as a potential "word-of-mouth" influencer to get everyone you know to try them out as well.

Travel light.

Don't bring a lot of preconceived notions about how solo diners, or even you as a solo diner, should be treated or will be treated. Be open to adventure. That empty chair across from you at the table next to the kitchen door might well be where the chef takes his or her break.

Finally, if you're reading this book, you're probably familiar with the very fickle New York restaurant scene. Today's hot ticket is tomorrow's "for rent" sign. All of the listings in this book were verified at press time. You'll want to call and confirm details. You can also check for updates at the official *Table for One* site, table-for-one.com. Happy solo dining!

About the Reviews

Price key:

$ = less than $20
$$ = $20 to $40
$$$ = $40 to $60
$$$$ = more than $60

Prices are per person (of course), including dessert and one glass of wine.

Rating Icons:

👨‍🍳 = Service
🛋 = Lighting
🍴 = Food
🍷 = Selection of wines by the glass
🪑 = comfort/placement/number of small tables suitable for solo diners

5 = superior
4 = very good
3 = good
2 = barely adequate
1 = abysmal

Note: the absence of a rating for wine selections means the establishment does not serve wine.

BELOW CANAL STREET
Chinatown, Tribeca, Wall Street

DOWNTOWN HUMS. There's the buzz of bulls and bears on Wall Street, the roar tunneling down canyons of tall buildings lining short crooked streets. There's the hubbub of tourists gawking at Chinatown, the Twin Towers, and South Street Seaport. There's City Hall, the Museum of the American Indian, and even Battery Park.

Opportunities for solo dining down here range from the very good to the very bad. Most restaurants in and around South Street Seaport handle tables for one well enough, if not well. The financial district caters to business lunches—two or more—and not the single diner.

Chinatown and Little Italy have their own peculiarities. In Chinatown, tables for ten abound. You can take your cue from that about how they feel about solo diners. Alas, that's often where the best food is, leaving the more usual tables for two or four to the tourist traps. Little Italy is lined with sidewalk cafés that cater to casual dining of any number at just about any time of day. The more serious restaurants tend to favor larger parties.

7

That said, there are gems to be found.

Bubby's
120 Hudson Street (North Moore Street)
212-219-0666

$ 🍴 🍴 🍴 🍴

🌱 🌱 🌱   🍷 🍷

🛎 🛎 🛎   🛍 🛍 🛍 🛍

This place is hell during weekend brunch. That said, it can also feel like heaven on weekdays and off hours. A favorite of famous Tribeca-ites like Harvey Keitel and Robert DeNiro, this very relaxed, soups-sandwiches-salads café is the ideal locale to settle in with something to read and savor a leisurely breakfast or lunch. Dress down, sit back, and you'll fit right in. The small, attractive bar serves a fine selection of beers but a small range of wines by the glass. P.S. Don't miss Bubby's made-from-scratch pies—they're legendary.

City Hall
131 Duane Street
212-227-7777

$ $ $ 🍴 🍴 🍴

🌱 🌱 🌱   🍷 🍷

🛎 🛎 🛎 🛎 🛎   🛍 🛍 🛍

No, not that City Hall. This is a downtown New York restaurant that makes a fetish of evoking what twenty-first-century investment bankers imagine New York restaurants were like in the Robber Baron and What's-Good-for-General-Motors eras. It's a huge art deco space with spectacular downtown views. The decor features photographs of old New York. As with any business-oriented establishment, you're always likely to find at least one other solo diner here. The retro menu ranges from iceberg lettuce salad and she-crab soup to steak and baked Alaska. The Solo Diner told you it was retro. The raw bar is excellent, and shellfish stews and pan roasts are prepared right before your eyes. That many offerings are for two—like a double steak—or more—plateau de fruits de mer—might explain the different readings solo diners get about their reception. Some find City Hall accessible; others find the reception carefully neutral. Think strategically. Points for excellent lighting.

Columbus Bakery

225 Liberty Street (Inside 2 World Financial Center)
212-945-9404
See page 101.

Cosi/Xando

3 World Financial Center
212-571-2001

54 Pine Street (at William Street)
212-809-2674

55 Broad Street (between Beaver Street and Exchange Place)
212-344-5000
$

By day it's Cosi. Like Starbucks and Au Bon Pain, you go to a counter, order something, and take out or find an empty table. Around 4:30 it becomes Xando. At certain locations (including these) it becomes a drinks and light supper place with table service. The daytime coffee, pastries, and sandwiches are much better than Starbucks, if not as good as Au Bon Pain's (which has the best food of the three ubiquitous chains and, despite the name, is the least pretentious about being a glorified cafeteria). And the java jockeys are much nicer. For better or worse, several of The Solo Diner's solo-dining friends recommended Cosi as the best place they knew for solo dining. In this neighborhood, in a certain price range, that may be the case.

Grace
114 Franklin Street (between West Broadway and Church)
212-343-4200

$ $

Though this elongated, airy place opened fairly recently, it's already become a neighborhood favorite—unpretentious, friendly, and eager to please. For solo diners, it offers a number of bonuses, including a forty-foot-long bar serving the full menu (inexpensive, Asian-accented fare like a pulled duck sandwich, seared tuna with sea vegetable salad, mussels, and chicken dumplings) and a good number of wines by the glass. Since the well-lighted bar tends to get crowded later in the evening, solo diners can savor elbow room while they graze and read at lunch or dinnertime. The bartenders can be harried when they double as servers, but they stay friendly and chatty.

Hudson River Club
4 World Financial Center
250 Vesey Street
212-786-1500

Hudson Valley wine and cuisine are served here in a cavernous room with a spectacular view of the marina. This is a serious business lunch place, more special occasion/romantic at dinner. Most of the daytime clientele are men. The men's club atmosphere might put off some solo diners, but The Solo Diner has always found the welcome here friendly and professional; the World Financial Center location means they're accustomed to lone travelers and solo business diners. The food is quite good, from grouse to rabbit potpie, from apple-pumpkin soup to lemon meringue pie. Wines by the glass are expensive, but the beer list is extensive. The solo diner, male or female, should think strategically.

Joe's Shanghai
9 Pell Street (between Bowery and Mott)
212-233-8888

$ $

It's not the decor or the service that makes Joe's Shanghai worth a visit. It's the Shanghai noodles and soup dumplings. A soup dumpling is a dumpling with pork or crab inside, served in a broth. Think Twinkie with nutritional value. The menu lists them as "steamed buns," but the proper name is xiao lung bao. Other worthwhile dishes include razorback clams in black bean sauce and chicken marinated in wine. Tables are for ten, but the staff is friendly. This is one of the few places for which The Solo Diner makes an exception to the "no communal tables" rule. No wine list, more like a beer menu. And the only beer The Solo Diner has ever seen here is Budweiser and Tsingtao.

Kitchenette

80 West Broadway (at Warren Street)

212-267-6740

$

This thimble of a restaurant feels more West Village than Tribeca. But that's Tribeca's gain. It's also yours if you're staying nearby or shopping the neighborhood, which is sort of the opposite of Restaurant Row. Kitchenette originally served breakfast and brunch only; its down-home, delicious food proved so popular that its hours have now been extended to cover lunch and dinner too, seven days a week. It practically embraces solo diners and draws more locals than tourists. Though unbearably packed at breakfast and lunch, the room settles down at dinnertime. Tasty "blue-plate specials" like sloppy joes and catfish round out a generous menu. Lighting could be better at night, but it's serviceable.

Lemongrass Grill

110 Liberty Street (at Church Street)

212-962-1370

$

Regardless of location, Lemongrass, which is a mini-chain, is a bit of a gamble. At its best, you'll get well-prepared, if tamed-for-round-eyes Thai food with reasonably good service. Other nights you'll get either bland food with good service or good food with bad service. At the very least, all locations are built to be solo diner friendly and highly efficient. The University Place branch, farther uptown, is the best of the lot. When the kitchen is cooking (so to speak), Lemongrass is a good introduction to the basic elements of Thai cuisine.

New Pasteur Restaurant

85 Baxter Street (between Bayard and Canal)
212-308-3656

$

The interior at this bright, compact Chinatown Vietnamese restaurant basically consists of communal tables. Still, The Solo Diner makes this place another exception to his communal table rule. Why? Addictive specialties (New York's best summer rolls with peanut sauce, tasty sugarcane shrimp, hearty phos, massive vegetarian bean-curd plate), low prices (few entrées top $10, most much less), earnest service, and terrific lighting. You'll have to rub elbows (literally) with a quirky collection of locals and tourists, but it's all part of the experience.

Nha Trang

87 Baxter Street (between Bayard and Canal)
212-233-5948

$

Pasteur's longtime next-door rival is equally solo-friendly. Like many of Chinatown's best restaurants, the appeal is food, not decor or ambience. Unlike many of Chinatown's best restaurants, Nha Trang offers Vietnamese, not Chinese, cuisine. Nha Trang is a well-lighted storefront that offers very good food at very good prices. At lunch the place is filled with solo diners—many of them jurors or other legal types from the courts nearby. Shrimp grilled on sugarcane, pho tai—a hearty soup filled with noodles and slices of beef—and Vietnamese coffee (a kind of café au lait made with heavily sweetened condensed milk) are good choices. But also unlike many of Chinatown's best restaurants, the staff will help you with the menu.

North Star Pub
South Street Seaport
93 South Street
212-509-6757
$ $
At first glance the North Star Pub looks like the typical "theme" eatery that plagues places like Harborplace in Baltimore, Faneuil Hall in Boston, and South Street Seaport in New York. And on one level, it is. It's a kind of British-style pub transplanted and reimagined for a tourist "destination" in New York. It's also a lot solo-friendlier than you'd expect. The crowd is a very convivial mix of British ex-pats and Anglophilic Americans, mostly working in and around Wall Street. Harp, Fuller, and Guinness on tap are the main draws here—not to mention some eighty-six single malt scotches. The food is better than it ought to be at a

theme place. Popular favorites include kidney pie, fish and chips, and shepherd's pie. Women alone, beware; major pickup action is attempted here.

Nyonya
194 Grand Street (between Mott and Mulberry)
212-334-3669
$ $

On good days this Malaysian restaurant is busy, rushed, and authentic, serving interesting, spicy food. Solo diners are served with the same brusque service groups of two or four get. On bad days it is busy, rushed, and bland; you'll get more authentic food at the tamed-for-New-Yorkers Penang. Despite having the appeal and ambience of a greasy spoon, the restaurant is popular in general and with New York's Malaysians in particular.

Odeon
145 West Broadway (between Duane and Thomas)
212-233-0507
$ $ $

Now entering its third decade, Odeon has defied all laws of restaurant gravity by remaining steadfastly hip, hot, and cool. People-watching is still an Olympic sport here, but it's not a scene like it used to be. That's good for solo diners; there's somewhat less of a commotion around the bar, where they serve the full menu and the lighting's good. Odeon deserves praise for remaining attitude-free; you'll get a friendly reception, a table if you want one (more likely off-peak), and earnest servers. The very consistent menu offers mostly fancified comfort food, like a pretty appetizer of yellow and red beefsteak tomatoes with mozzarella, a fat crab cake, and grilled portobello mushrooms. Among the entrées, you can't go wrong with the roasted half chicken with spinach and mashed potatoes, or the sea bass or grilled tuna (but repeat the word "rare" loud and slow). There's a stingy selection of wines by the glass, but you can order champagne that way.

Palacinka

28 Grand Street (between Thompson Street and Sixth Avenue)

212-625-0362

$

A palacinka, according to one of the waiters here, is a kind of crepe that originated "in Central Europe." Apparently, much of the odd ersatz-emigré decor (yellowed photos, old suitcases) arrived from the same part of the world. That said, Palacinka also follows through on the European café tradition of treating solo diners well. This diminutive, rough-yet-refined spot includes a number of small tables where solo diners can feel comfortable; though late evening can get very crowded, snagging a seat is very easy at more strategic hours. The menu, as astute readers may have guessed, is all about crepes: chicken crepes, vegetable crepes, Gruyère-and-tomato crepes, Nutella crepes, butter-and-sugar crepes. The pancakes on the outside are thin and flavorful, and the fillings are rich and generous. Fair selection of wines by the glass; lighting is adequate. *Paper* magazine, the style bible, calls Palacinka the "best place to mope on a rainy day"; The Solo Diner says it's the place you're most likely to see diners reading Kafka.

Pepolino

281 West Broadway (between Canal and Lispenard)
212-966-9983

$ $ $

A friend of The Solo Diner's who hails from Florence says this is the most authentic Italian eatery in New York. It certainly feels that way, with a rustic, woody interior up a short flight of stairs and a menu of simple, earthy specialties from all over the Old Country. The Solo Diner loved the yellow pepper soup, rich bread soup, grilled swordfish, and perfect pastas. There's a warm welcome at the door, and a handsome waitstaff that loves taking time to engage customers in casual conversation. The place never gets packed, so scoring a table isn't usually a problem, even at peak hours. Lighting is terrific, including at night.

Petite Abeille

134 West Broadway (between Duane and Reade)
212-791-1360

$ $

From the minute they opened, these Belgian cafés felt like they'd been part of their neighborhoods for years (see additional listings on pages 51 and 84). While each location's different (14th Street offers table service, this one and the one on Hudson are more counter-service-oriented), they're all godsends for solo diners. Comfortable small tables and window-side stools, terrific lighting, friendly service, and simple, delicious Eurofood (including NYC's tastiest waffles) make them terrific places for a quick snack or a long, leisurely meal. There's charming, quirky decor in each spot, including French children's book covers on the wall and prices in Belgian francs on the menu. Note: the 14th Street location is open 24 hours daily; 18th Street serves until early evening most nights.

Pizzeria Uno Chicago
South Street Seaport
89 South Street
212-791-7999
$

During off hours here, at the culinary-challenged South Street Seaport, a solo diner is likely to be seated at a booth that would be used to accommodate six during the midday and after-work crushes. A caveat, however: at peak hours solo diners are likely to be ignored in favor of "larger parties," and given tables near the kitchen or at the bar. When The Solo Diner pointed this out, he was told it was "policy." As for the rest, this noisy, theme-decorated national chain offers deep-dish pizza made with traditional and nontraditional ingredients. The pizzas tend to be greasy, but the spinoccoli works. Anything that can't be characterized as pizza or bar food should be avoided. The hunger you see in the eyes of the crowd at the bar is not just for food.

Sweet-n-Tart Café

76 Mott Street (at Canal Street)
212-334-8088

20 Mott Street (between Chatham Square and
Pell Street)
212-964-0380
$ 𝆑 𝆑 𝆑 𝆑

And now for something completely different: these hopping
little places specialize in tong shui—sweet Chinese health
"tonics" believed to have healthful effects. Lotus seeds,
gingko, and nuts are some of the less exotic ingredients. If
the good-looking, mostly Asian crowd here is any indica-
tion, the drinks work. The menu also includes Hong Kong
snacks, soups, congees, noodles, and rice dishes. The places
themselves are clean, white-tiled, well-lit, and offer small
tables ideal for solo diners. Huge crowds, especially on
weekends, are the only drawback. Good lighting; no alcohol served.

Tiffin

18 Murray Street (between Broadway and Church)
212-791-3510
$ $ 𝆑 𝆑 𝆑 𝆑 𝆑

This sibling of Thali (see page 58) and Tikka (see page 88)
offers very tasty vegetarian fare in a bright, airy, relaxed
room with exposed brick and billowing drapes. It's also

Celebrity Sound Bite

I frequently breakfast solo. My favorite place is the Frontier Diner at 39th Street and Third Avenue, just a block from my apartment. I have a favorite waitress there named Chris and I know everybody in the place. Breakfast is a big treat for me.

If I were dining alone, I'd probably go to Chin Chin on East 49th and order their Grand Marnier Shrimp. To eat out in New York by yourself you need to establish rapport and frequent the same places where they are used to seeing you and like you. After all, you are taking up solo a lot of space.

—Liz Smith
veteran syndicated columnist and author of
Natural Blonde, a Memoir (Hyperion Books)

very welcoming of solo diners. Even though there are few tables for one per se, the hosts are unfailingly accommodating, and The Solo Diner has never had trouble getting seated, even at a four-top. You'll find some familiar favorites on the menu, along with unconventional fare like Jaipuri Khazana (fruits and vegetables in curry sauce) and Bhara Khumb (roasted portobello mushrooms filled with cottage cheese). Invaluable if you're staying or working down here; worth a trip if you're not. No wine, but beer is served.

Walker's

16 North Moore Street (at Varick Street)

212-941-0142

$

Before many uptowners even knew where Tribeca was, Walker's was welcoming locals with dependable comfort food like burgers and chicken. The surrounding area has trendified permanently, but Walker's soldiers on, and solo diners should be thankful. You won't get warmer treatment anywhere, even if it's your first time. Yes, waitstaff can be quirky, but they're always charming and a big part of the appeal here. Lighting's fine, and the full menu's served at the imposing old bar too. Settle in to one of the checked-tablecloth-covered tables and enjoy a quintessential New York experience. P.S. For the morbidly curious, the late JFK Junior and his wife lived next door at 20 North Moore.

Zutto

77 Hudson Street (between Jay and Harrison)

212-233-3287

$ $

An oasis on a very quiet stretch of Hudson Street, Zutto has been offering top-quality sushi and sashimi for years, going back to the days when Tribeca still felt undiscovered. The fish here is still excellent, the service very efficient, and tables for one plentiful (along with the sushi bar, of course). The setting's also remarkably relaxing and unkitschy. Because of its standards and location, this is one of only four sushi bars included in *Table for One*. Few wines by the glass, but there's a huge selection of sake to make up for it. P.S. Zutto recently opened a West Village location (62 Greenwich Avenue, 212-229-1796).

CANAL STREET TO 14TH STREET

Lower East Side, SoHo, West Village, East Village

BOBOS, ACCORDING TO the author David Brooks, are bourgeois bohemians, middle-class and upper-middle-class people who are involved with the information age culture industry, turning ideas into products. As traditional artistic/bohemian enclaves succumb to gentrification, that's exactly who can afford to live in SoHo, Greenwich Village, the East Village, and even the Lower East Side.

Still, on the one hand, with students from three universities—New York University, The New School for Social Research, and Cooper Union—and on the other, refugees from punk and the summer of love, plenty of genteel, impoverished artistic types remain for local character.

There are also active Asian and Latino communities in what used to be the northern hump of the Lower East Side and Alphabet City. And then there is Sixth Street in the East Village, a Little India with such single-friendly ethnic eateries as Passage to India (308 East 6th Street), Balaka (318 East 6th), Shah Bagh (328 East 6th), and Gandhi (345 East 6th).

SoHo may be New York's worst neighborhood for solo diners. The see-and-be-seen places want crowded tables, to seem to be where important people go and where important things happen. The West Village and the East Village still cater to traditional bohemian solos, but the choice is often obscure, ethnic restaurants or coffeehouses. The area has the city's only Burmese restaurant, and if you don't know where Chumley's is, you're not going to find it (86 Bedford Street; look for the small unmarked Alice-in-Wonderland door). In general, these places have good food at good prices, but how about a little decor and atmosphere?

Anglers & Writers

420 Hudson Street (at St. Luke's Place)
212-675-0810

$ $ 🍴 🍴 🍴

If there were an award for the restaurant most supportive of a solo diner through thick and thin (crowds, that is), Anglers & Writers would win hands down. A friend of The Solo Diner's arranged to meet a blind date there. He arrived a bit early, took a table, and waited for the woman to show up. And waited for the woman to show up. And waited. And waited. About all Anglers & Writers did was give him a nice comforting cup of tea and didn't bother him, even though a flurry of activity would have made his table useful. No, the woman never showed up. Yes, he did leave a very big tip. And while all he got was a cup of tea, Anglers & Writers got a lifetime customer and booster. Idiosyncratic and serene, the tearoom affects the look of an early twentieth-century fishing lodge by way of English country style. Think Ernest Hemingway meets Mary Emmerling. The staff is obviously terribly nice. However, the food might be best described as not without charm. It's the usual, but decently prepared, American tearoom specialties of tea and cakes, supplemented by carefully prepared soups, salads, and sandwiches.

Aquagrill
210 Spring Street (at Sixth Avenue)
212-274-0505
$ $ $

A small, cool, and casual SoHo neighborhood seafood place with a terrace, blue and yellow "undersea" decor, and candlelight. The bar near the entrance is ideal for solo diners; the full menu is served. The nautical memorabilia scattered about may be fake, but the food is first-rate. Well-priced, interesting dishes include seared scallops with a crabmeat polenta. A little overburdened at peak hours, and there's an appreciable romantic undertone. But solo diners here get a warm welcome, especially for SoHo.

B&H Vegetarian Restaurant
127 Second Avenue (between 7th Street and St. Mark's Place)
212-505-8065
$

Celebrity Sound Bite

I eat alone often because my job is to talk and I get burned out of talking sometimes and would just like to sit with a nice meal and read and brainstorm. The best place to eat is at the bar, sushi or traditional, because bartenders are the most knowledgeable people in the restaurant business because they are forced to interface with the customer. Gramercy Tavern has great food, great service, and the room is so busy that you can eat alone without having people look at you and say, "Oh, look at that poor lonely guy who doesn't have a date!"

I eat at the bar at Bond Street (6 Bond Street; 212-777-2500) downtown, Bottino (246 Tenth Avenue; 212-206-6766) in Chelsea, Coffee Shop in Union Square (where I watch the Knicks games), and Campagna (24 East 21st Street; 212-460-0900).

That is the other great thing about dining alone . . . I can focus on my Knicks without being rude to my guest by looking over his or her shoulder and saying, "Yeah, sure, yeah."

—Jason McCabe Calacannis
founder/editor-in-chief, *Silicon Alley Reporter*
siliconalleyreporter.com

The minuscule "restaurant" is actually a bright, very busy counter with a few small tables lining the opposite wall. It's been a neighborhood refuge for solo diners longer than The Solo Diner can remember. At night it can feel like an Edward Hopper painting, but that's part of the charm. The food can be delicious; skip nouveau additions like veggie burgers and go for the real thing—traditional favorites like latkes, knishes, killer borscht, and mushroom barley soup. Service is efficient, but cold; the young servers don't warm up to you until you're well-established as a regular. If you don't feel like making small talk, just observe the flow of customers, a gallery of every type that makes this neighborhood so fascinating. This is one place where the counter's the prime seating area.

The Bagel Restaurant
170 West 4th Street (between Cornelia and Jones)
212-255-0106
$

Now that it's been colonized by middlebrow clothing chains and overpriced coffee purveyors, it's easy to forget how idiosyncratic the West Village used to be. Luckily, there are places like The Bagel around to remind us. Owned by the same family since the sixties, and constantly packed with many solo regulars, this shoe-box-size joint basically serves breakfast fare and coffee shop staples. But what fabulous fare it is: perfectly grilled burgers, well-turned-out eggs and pancakes, and, of course, above-average bagels, which are served with almost everything. Coffee's tasty too. Servers are of the old-fashioned "Enjoy it, honey!" variety and seem to respect the long tradition of solo dining behind this place. Lighting is excellent. Claustrophobics take note: you may have to sit closer than you'd like to your neighbors.

Benny's Burritos
113 Greenwich Avenue (at Jane Street)
212-727-3560
93 Avenue A (East 6th Street)
212-254-2054

Cheap, cute, beloved neighborhood hangouts, both Benny's have long given solo diners a warm (and spicy) welcome; you definitely won't be the only one here on your own. Ignore the dime-store decor and focus on the massive plates of Mexican food that keeps these places packed. As an added attraction, both locations offer primo people-watching. Avenue A features the East Village parade of the pierced, tattooed, and dyed; Greenwich Avenue offers a diverting mix of Chelsea boys, West Village natives, and lost tourists.

Bereket Turkish Kebab House
187 East Houston Street (at Orchard Street)
212-425-7700

One of the characteristics of this place that draws gripes—supernova-bright lighting, twenty-four hours a day—is one of the reasons The Solo Diner loves stopping by when he's on the Lower East Side. For one thing, most of the other restaurants in the neighborhood are loungey scene spots so dark you can't even see the menu; to boot, very few of them are solo-friendly. Bereket might not offer much in the way of ambience—it's just a half-step up from a cafeteria—but you can walk in here at any hour with your book or newspaper, chat with the friendly counter help, order delicious, fresh-made Turkish meat or vegetarian dishes (shish kebabs, Turkish sandwiches, white bean salad), and watch the demimonde go by on Houston Street at your table for one.

Black & White

86 East 10th Street (between Third and Fourth Avenues)

212-253-0246

$ $

Because the owners of Niagara and Spy Bar opened Black & White a year ago, locals and reviewers have been wondering about when an annoying door policy would start and when the waitstaff would become insufferable. Instead, it has so far been a kind of local place where the chef wanders out to the bar for a quick chat with a friend who's dropped by, the waitress remembers you like the one table with light, and the bartender turns a blind eye to the dog sitting quietly at his master's feet at the bar. The food is quite good; The Solo Diner adores the soups. Earlier is bet-

ter. More important, because Black & White seats so few
people, here is where the solo diner who smokes might
wish to dine.

Café de Bruxelles
118 Greenwich Avenue (at West 13th Street)
212-206-1830

$ $

Café de Bruxelles has been a refuge for solo diners for
years. While seating in the main dining room of this trian-
gular West Village haunt is quite possible, the tiny tables
near the zinc bar are more appealing. You wind up think-
ing you're really in some old cathedral town in Northern
Europe, if not Belgium itself. The beer list is better than
the wine list, with the emphasis on European brews in general and Belgian beers in particular. Lighting is fine for reading and a bit better in the dining room than in the bar. The
menu highlights Belgian cuisine in both its glory and its
oddity; the moule et frites and carbonnade flamanade are
excellent, possibly the best in New York.

Café Loup
105 West 13th Street (between Sixth and Seventh
Avenues)
212-255-4746

$ $ $

Any place that can seat The Solo Diner on a Saturday night without a reservation earns his undying gratitude. Café Loup has done it with a smile. Even better, the host and servers here treat him like a regular, which he is not by any stretch. A tasteful, subdued room with paintings and photographic works from the owners' private collection on the walls, Café Loup serves cleaned-up-classic versions of French favorites, with an emphasis on fish and game (the meaty yellowfin tuna entrée, served rare, is a favorite). A wonderfully chosen wine list, with many selections by the glass, rounds out a terrific solo-dining experience. Plenty of small tables, adequate lighting. P.S. Lots of celebrities come here to dine without being harassed.

Café Mogador
101 St. Mark's Place (between First and Second Avenues)
212-677-2226
$

Years ago, when The Solo Diner first dined at Café Mogador, it was a narrow, virtually undecorated restaurant in what was the dicier end of St. Mark's. Close to two decades later, the restaurant has easily doubled in size and the area seems a lot less dicey, what with the East Village having moved farther east. Mogador offers Moroccan cuisine—good, but not great—in a setting that falls somewhere between minimal and funky. The Solo Diner likes the tagine with prunes and apricots. The other tagines—a kind of stew served over couscous—are good to decent as well. Service is more amiable than professional, and singles are welcome at any time. Lighting is good for reading, and the last time The Solo Diner was at Mogador, the staff seemed cool about letting people sit and read.

Café Rafaella

134 Seventh Avenue South (between Charles and 10th Streets)

212-929-7247

$

When this local haunt added generous sandwiches, salads, pastas, and crepes to their usual fare of coffee drinks, teas, and desserts, The Solo Diner became a regular (he loves the Rafaella Salad, with grilled chicken, artichoke hearts, and a mountain of greens). Warm and welcoming in winter, an oasis in summer, Café Rafaella offers an ideal setting to read, think, and people-watch as you dine. Since they're so accustomed to solo diners, the waitstaff here are accommodating, if not always friendly; they're also maddeningly slow at times. The interior here is darkish, but individual lamps beside each table make reading easy; there's an abundance of small tables, but beware of a few Lilliputian tables for two that leave room for an espresso or a magazine, but not both. Decor is early flea market. In warm weather, tourists and locals alike queue up for the primo outdoor seating to take in the endless, Felliniesque parade of West Village characters.

Cedar Tavern

82 University Place (between 11th and 12th Streets)

212-741-9574

It's hard for The Solo Diner to dislike a place that will use a booth that can seat four as a table for one. If the Cedar Tavern has the room, they'll give you any table you want. This place also has a long history as a neighborhood hangout for artists and students. In fact, local luminaries like Jackson Pollock, Willem de Kooning, Mark Rothko, Allen Ginsberg, Jack Kerouac, and Gregory Corso all hung out here in days of yore, and Dylan himself was reputed to have dropped in occasionally. Cedar Tavern still oozes atmosphere and even hosts readings on Sundays. Older eyes might find the lighting too dim to do their own reading over dinner, but the noise level isn't too bad for this kind of place. Service can be vague; even dawdlers may find waiting to be served or for the check a frustrating experience. Food is inexpensive and generally reliable—try the pork chops or hamburgers. Wine list is very respectable.

Chez Brigitte

77 Greenwich Avenue (between Bank Street and
Seventh Avenue South)

212-929-6736

When the history of solo dining is written, the name Chez Brigitte will loom large. Founded in 1958, this eleven-seat gem has changed hands only once and still serves the same sophisticated, delectable homemade meals to faithful followers at insanely low prices. The atmosphere is so congenial you'll feel you've dropped in on a friend who happened to be cooking. Do like the natives do: get your newspaper next door, grab one of the counter seats—there are no others—and dig into daily specials like roast leg of lamb, veal stew, or roast beef. Save room for the homemade desserts.

Christine's
208 First Avenue (between 12th and 13th Streets)
212-254-2474

$

An East Village institution, Christine's is the kind of place where solo diners often outnumber couples and groups. If you're looking for atmosphere, forget it; the place falls somewhere between a VFW hall and a doctor's waiting room. But for warm service and superb Polish favorites at ludicrously low prices, few places come close. Irresistible soups, blintzes, pierogis, kielbasa; all-day breakfast. Excellent lighting.

Col Legno
231 East 9th Street (between Second and Third Avenues)
212-777-4650

$ $

There's something odd and appealing about this sparse, quiet Tuscan Italian restaurant on a relatively quiet East Village block. For one thing, the fifteen or so tables are extremely well-spaced, a rarity around here; for another, the wood-burning oven in the back occupies an airy, high-ceilinged room that could seat another thirty diners. There are quite a few small tables, the lighting's soft but adequate for reading, and the simple, clean food (including a splendid rosemary roasted chicken) is delicious and honest. A couple of wines are available by the glass, along with beer. P.S. You won't see many tourists here.

Cosi/Xando
504 Avenue of the Americas (at 13th Street)
212-462-4188
See page 9.

Cowgirl Hall of Fame
519 Hudson Street (West 10th Street)
212-633-1133

$ $

The decor here puts the "kitsch" into "kitchen," but it's so over the top with its cowgirl theme that you fall under the campy spell. The place is friendly to the point of being in your face, but be aware that it's also a favorite for parties and groups. The food is a New York gloss on Southern trailer park cooking: fried chicken, corn dogs, Frito pie, and the like. There's even a deliberately tacky souvenir shop and free copies of a local paper that lists places for country and western music and dancing. The Solo Diner must confess that while he had a perfectly satisfactory single-dining experience here, the tendency is to go when meeting friends who are bringing the kids. If your tolerance for "kitsch and kids" is low, you'll do better elsewhere.

Dojo

14 West 4th Street (between Broadway and Mercer)
212-505-8394

24–26 St. Mark's Place (between Second and Third Avenues)
212-674-9821

$ 🍴🍴🍴

4️⃣ 🍸🍸🍸

🪑🪑🪑🪑 🪑🪑🪑🪑🪑

The Solo Diner has been coming to these happening, sort-of-vegetarian spots since his school days, and he still does a double take every time he glances at the menu. Can the food still be that cheap? Prices haven't changed much since the eighties, and neither has the simple decor or college-kid attitude. No matter how busy it gets here—and during the school year it's mobbed—The Solo Diner's always been given a table, even with couples and groups behind him. Favorites here include fresh, tasty stir-fries, meal-sized Japanese soba noodle soups, and simple grilled or steamed fish with veggies and rice. Zero ambience, but no one comes here for that. Service, however, is a major drawback here (for everyone, not just solo diners); servers act like they wish they were in a different profession, or maybe a different city. Bar serves a decent selection of beer and wines by the glass.

Dolphins

35 Cooper Square (between 5th and 6th Streets)
212-357-9195

$ $ 🍴 🍴 🍴 🍴

👤 👤 👤 👤   🍷 🍷 🍷

🍺 🍺 🍺   🪑 🪑

Dolphins was the only restaurant The Solo Diner went to where the waitperson suggested he might wish to taste the wine before she poured the glass. Little details like that go a long way. Shame it didn't get as far as the hostess, who insisted on seating The Solo Diner in the back and seemed to resent having to walk that far. The food, mostly fish, is excellent; the service is polite, professional, and well-paced; and the light, although flattering, will not induce eyestrain. The food is extremely well-prepared at Dolphins, but it's more memorable in totality: you have a sense of having dined well without necessarily remembering any dish that stands out as brilliantly conceived. The Solo Diner found the lobster bisque velvety and subtle, and the crab cakes worth going back for.

Drovers Tap Room

9 Jones Street

212-627-1233

$ $ 🍴 🍴 🍴

👤 👤 👤   🍷 🍷

🍺 🍺   🪑 🪑 🪑

Drovers Tap Room draws customers—many of them solo—from all over town. The place is not that big, so it's best to come early or late. This is the sort of place you go for fried chicken or London broil. It's the sort of place that serves only New York beers and then only on tap. And it's the sort of place you get well-prepared comfort food served in what is supposed to be out-to-town ambience; this is what one imagines neighborhood restaurants feel like in Boston or Philadelphia.

EJ's Luncheonette

432 Avenue of the Americas (between 9th and 10th Streets)

212-473-5555

For some reason, The Solo Diner finds root beer on tap funny. There is no accounting for taste. This local mini-chain is part of the comfort-food-in-retro-decor fashion that currently plagues New York. The food all too accurately recreates the circa 1950s diner/luncheonette the decor echoes. It is also both kid and solo diner friendly. EJ's can be quite noisy from the stroller and cell phone set. Weekend brunches get hectic; weekdays are calmer, and solo diners can usually snag a spacious booth with little fuss.

Elephant and Castle

66 Greenwich Avenue (near Seventh Avenue Santa and West 11th Street)

212-243-1400

Cozy, slightly faded, and idiosyncratic (the tiny bathroom is through swinging doors in the kitchen), Elephant and Castle is a throwback to the old Greenwich Village, when cafés and coffee shops ruled the landscape and solo diners had an embarrassment of riches to choose from. An abundance of small tables includes choice seats where you'd least expect them—like the two-tops opposite the kitchen.

Inventive omelettes are the trademark here; the daily special might include pesto, cheddar, apples, nuts, vegetables, or any combination thereof. For lunch and dinner the basics are most reliable, including burgers and a Caesar salad so good it's got a cult following. The servers here are used to solo diners and treat them warmly, even if they're not part of the crew of regulars. Lighting is ideal during the day, adequate at night, and better in the front of the restaurant than in the back.

Fanelli's Café
94 Prince Street (at Mercer Street)
212-431-5744
$ $

Thank God for Fanelli's, one of the last outposts of SoHo realness in a neighborhood that looks increasingly like a mall. It's also one of the few places where solo diners won't feel out of place in these parts. The Solo Diner's favorite tables are on the left just as you walk in the main room. Don't be put off by the seedy exterior and very basic decor (complete with red-checked tablecloths); savor instead the old wooden furnishings and dig into the generous burgers, chili, meat loaf, and other staples. P.S. Nonsmokers beware: smoking is still permitted in here. Active bar scene, which female solo diners should bear in mind.

Florent
69 Gansevoort Street (between Greenwich and Washington Streets)
212-989-5779

$ $ 🍴 🍴 🍴

👤 👤 👤   Y Y Y

🛏 🛏 🛏 🛏 🛏   🪑 🪑 🪑 🪑 🪑

Sure, the neighborhood's chic now. But when Florent first opened its doors in 1985 (twenty-four hours a day!) the nearby streets were a desolate landscape of warehouses and abandoned cars. Florent's no longer the only kid on the block, but it's still the best, and an absolute treat for solo diners. The interior is ablaze with fluorescent lights; the red vinyl banquettes are a great place to dine, read, and people-watch; and the long counter is an appealing alternative to joining the crowd. But what a crowd; at any given hour, you'll see models and photographers on breaks from photo shoots, men and women in black tie, leathermen and/or clubgoers coming down from a long night of partying—sometimes at the same table. You might even see owner and indomitable spirit Florent Morellet traipse through the room. Food runs the gamut from omelettes, Salad Niçoise, and a half chicken with mashed potatoes (very good) to fish specials, couscous, pastas (OK), and steak au poivre (avoid at all costs). Service ranges from friendly to spacey (The Solo Diner knew of a waiter here who was a well-known New York drag queen). Full bar with good selection of wines by the glass.

French Roast

78 West 11th Street (at Sixth Avenue)
212-533-2233

$ $ 🍴 🍴 🍴

👤 👤   Y Y Y

🛏 🛏   🪑 🪑 🪑 🪑

Like L'Express in Manhattan South, this mini-chain is a very New York gloss on a French bistro. It could also be described as a French bistro rethought as a twenty-four-hour diner. Food is good to adequate; simple fare like omelettes are your best bet. Service comes with an attitude, but they will almost always accommodate a solo diner just about any time of day. Or night. If you're on your own for a very early breakfast or very late snack, these places make a perfect choice.

Gotham Bar & Grill

123 East 12th Street (between Fifth Avenue and University Place)

212-620-4020

$ $ $ $

The Solo Diner can't imagine a more sublime experience than lunch or dinner here. A plush seat at the long, immaculate bar beats a table almost anywhere else (a good thing, since tables are still tough tickets here after fifteen years). Even on a frenzied weekend night, the unflappable hosts have always managed to seat The Solo Diner with a smile. Unfailingly courteous and warm bartenders double as your waiters, and the "counter" serves the same superb selection as the main dining room, abuzz behind you in a gigantic, sunken space. Perfect lighting for readers, all the better to see beautifully presented plates like yellowfin tuna tartare, seared loin of venison, or sautéed skate wings. And there's an expertly chosen list of wines by the glass to boot.

Gus' Place

149 Waverly Place (between Christopher Street and Sixth Avenue)

212-645-8511

$ $

Since this place is tucked into a wedge of Waverly Place that feels hidden from the rest of the West Village, it rarely attracts the crowds and tourists that descend on other neighborhood establishments. That would be enough to make Gus' a perfect choice for a table for one, but the food, service, and laid-back Greek-taverna atmosphere enhance a terrific solo-dining experience. Enjoy the view from a table beside the floor-to-ceiling windows and dig into juicy charred octopus stewed in red wine, meaty grilled tuna with white beans, rich couscous dishes, and a killer Greek antipasto plate. Desserts are familiar but well-prepared, like baklava or fresh fruit with homemade yogurt and honey. Small selection of wines by the glass, but Greek wines anywhere are a rare pleasure. Service is warm, attentive, and professional; lighting's subtle but sufficient; and there are plenty of well-placed small tables. A treat that's worth the trip downtown.

Housing Works Used Books Café

126 Crosby Street (between Houston and Prince Streets)
212-334-3324

$

Because it's on a dreary block just slightly off the SoHo tourist path, this quiet, atmospheric bookstore-café never gets too crowded, even on weekends. That alone would make it a find for solo diners in need of a break from the downtown whirl. The fact that it offers delicious pastas, soups, sandwiches, desserts, coffees, and teas is almost a bonus; that the library-like bilevel space is perfectly lit for reading (of course) is icing on the cake. The men and women at the food counter are cheerful and unfailingly polite, and all of them seem to have taken serious training in espresso and cappuccino making. Almost every table here is perfect for solo diners, who can also take food and drink to tiny tables in the upstairs stacks. Best of all, proceeds from the shop benefit Housing Works, which helps HIV-positive homeless people. P.S. There's a surprisingly well-chosen list of wines by the glass to go with your lunch or light dinner here.

In Padella

145 Second Avenue (between 9th and 10th Streets)
212-598-9800

$ $

It's a little darker in here than The Solo Diner would like. Otherwise, In Padella is a relaxing spot for a cheap meal that feels anything but. Even when the expansive, rustic-feeling dining room gets crowded, the waitstaff seems to keep its head; there's a good-natured charm that permeates throughout the place. After you've checked out the pots that are hanging on the brick walls, turn your attention to the menu. There, you'll find straightforward favorites like tuna carpaccio, steamed artichoke, and grilled portobello mushroom appetizers, along with entrées like spaghetti with seafood, chicken cacciatore, and veal Milanese, all presented without surprises but with earthy flair. Pastas are perfectly prepared, and portions are generous. Modest but enjoyable wine list; laid-back, local crowd. The solo dining choice of *Table for One* celebrity Michael Musto!

Jerry's

101 Prince Street (between Greene and Mercer)

212-966-9464

$ $

In a "scene" neighborhood like SoHo, where solo diners can feel marooned, Jerry's offers a relaxed alternative. No matter how packed it gets in this white, bright nouveau diner—and The Solo Diner has witnessed some Potemkin-like crowd scenes here—the waitstaff has never been less than accommodating, often downright friendly. The dining room mostly includes banquettes and small tables, so solo diners are happily seated. The full menu—simple and hearty soups, sandwiches, salads, pastas—is served at the counter, whose only disadvantage is its proximity to the kitchen and servers' stations. Avoid the stroller-gridlocked weekend brunch. P.S. This was for years the SoHo art world's commissary, where people like Leo Castelli had regular tables, but that crowd's since moved on to West Chelsea, where Jerry's recently opened Jerry's Bar and Grill (470 West 23rd Street at 10th Avenue; 212-989-8456). It's large and attractive, but much less solo-friendly.

Katz's Delicatessen

205 East Houston Street (at Ludlow Street)

212-254-2246

"I'll have what she's having." With those words (and some help from Meg Ryan), Katz's entered the popular consciousness as one of the stars of *When Harry Met Sally*. Among New Yorkers, of course, the place was legendary long before that, as the "Send A Salami to Your Boy in the Army" posters attest. The surrounding neighborhood may have changed since then, but Katz's remains stubbornly, thankfully the same. The out-of-this-world pastrami still induces euphoria, and the (now multinational) countermen still dish classic New York attitude. Katz's setup is basically a large, fluorescent-lit cafeteria, with a long counter where patrons order colossal sandwiches, juicy hot dogs, famous egg creams, and less notable fare. You'll feel your arteries harden as you chew, but it's worth it. There are rows and rows of Formica tables which usually offer plenty of room for solo diners to enjoy their own space. Beer is available.

Knickerbocker's Bar and Grill
33 University Place (at 9th Street)
212-228-8490

In a city that seems to specialize in restaurants catering to a young crowd trying to make the scene, Knickerbocker's stands out as a place where the forty-something crowd can feed and relax. Even on busy nights you can see many tables for one. It's been around for years, essentially as the local "good" restaurant with steaks, a good bar, and jazz, but the food happens to be excellent (if not exactly innovative) and the staff handles everything with aplomb.

La Paella

214 East 9th Street (between First and Second Avenues)
212-598-4321

$ $

This tapas-size tapas bar in the East Village is about the square footage of a typical New York apartment. It's either cozy or cramped, depending upon your point of view. The Solo Diner was surprised that in a restaurant with so few tables, service was attentive and polite (and often quite stunning). There are at least four riojas by the glass, among other, less obvious Spanish choices, and the tapas themselves are tasty. Tables—larger than a mouse pad, but not much— and lighting are not user-friendly for solo diners who like to read while they eat.

Le Gamin

536 East 5th Street (between Avenues A and B)
212-254-8409

50 MacDougal Street (between Houston and Prince)
212-254-4678

$ $

Any place that features an overloaded magazine rack is OK with The Solo Diner, and these Franco-*New Yorkais* places (with a third branch in Chelsea) deliver the goods. They're practically designed for solo diners, so tables for one abound; at breakfast sometimes there are only solo travelers here, devouring their newspapers along with brioches and café au lait. The rest of the menu is serviceable and dependable, including salads, sandwiches, and crepes. P.S. If the staff gets snooty, maintain eye contact. They'll back down.

Lemongrass Grill
80 University Place (at 11th Street)
212-604-9870

37 Barrow Street (at Seventh Avenue South)
212-242-0606

53 Avenue A (between 3rd and 4th Streets)
212-674-3538
See page 12.

Lupe's East L.A. Kitchen
110 Sixth Avenue (at Watts Street)
212-966-1326

$

The Solo Diner has a fond memory of Lupe's: this is where he sat out his Senior Ball in college. He had decided to skip the big event, wandered all the way downtown from Columbia U., and ended up at a table for one at this Mexican cheapie on SoHo's western fringe. It felt like dining in someone's not-at-all-upscale living room, and that's exactly what he needed. Lupe's still has that feeling; it continues to dish up inexpensive, delicious burritos and enchiladas along with favorites like huevos rancheros, tamales, chili relleño, and pollo norteño (grilled chicken breast with onions and chilies) at *muy bien* prices. Irresistible flan and peanut butter cookies round out the dessert menu. Service is efficient but warm; lighting is adequate. Crowd includes fiercely loyal regulars and lots of area workers at lunchtime. Beer is available. Trivia buffs, take note: apparently, this is the place where Jeff Daniels dines and dashes at the beginning of Jonathan Demme's *Something Wild*.

Moustache

90 Bedford Street (between Barrow and Grove)
212-229-2220

265 East 10th Street (between First Avenue and Avenue A)
212-228-2022

$

You can get falafel, babaganoush, and the like anywhere in Manhattan. But the fare at Moustache is so fresh, the vibe so friendly, and the setting so mellow that these places have developed their own following. Best of all, their signature "pitzas"—pitas topped with unusual pizza fixings like lamb—make perfect meals for solo diners. Tables for one are a staple at both locations; the pocket-size West Village storefront is slightly out of the way, so you have a better chance of scoring a table there during peak hours, but the East 10th Street branch has a small outdoor garden that's a pleasure in warm weather. Lighting's terrific at both East and West; decor in both is clean, spare, and comfortable.

Next Door Nobu

105 Hudson Street (at Franklin Street)

212-334-4445

$ $ $

The Solo Diner can't imagine dining solo at the churning spectacle that is Nobu. But what a difference a door makes. Come around six or 6:30 and you'll all but have its adjacent sibling all to yourself. As for the food, Nobu Next Door tries to be something more than Nobu Lite and forges its own identity with a stronger emphasis on fish and sushi, while still maintaining the Asian-Latino fusion of its older sibling. It even offers many of the same dishes. Downside: unlike its namesake, Next Door Nobu doesn't take reservations. The result is a long first come, first served line at the door. Ninety-minute waits are not unheard of.

Noho Star

330 Lafayette Street (at Bleecker Street)

212-925-0070

$ $

Poor little Noho Star. It tries so hard to be hip. Instead it gets local artists and writers, families with children, Internet entrepreneurs discussing their futures, and a great number of solo diners. And it welcomes them all. The cuisine is Asian fusion/American with some Chinese offerings after six P.M. The soups are particularly good and The Solo Diner has slowly been turning kith and kin on to Noho

Star's wonderful crab cakes. Lighting is good, but it can be noisy when the place is full. Service is more amiable than professional, which no one minds, since most of the room is filled with regulars. When The Solo Diner worked in the neighborhood, this was his hangout, retreat, and occasional conference room.

Pearl Oyster Bar
18 Cornelia Street (between West 4th Street and Bleecker)
212-691-8211
$ $

Once this minuscule, idiosyncratic West Villager fills up, usually as early as seven P.M., forget it; you'll end up cooling your heels on the sidewalk with the rest of the hopeful crowd. But for an early dinner, this old-fashioned but up-to-the-minute place is a charmer. Sit at the counter rather than one of the few cramped tables. The saucy, funny servers are kind to solo diners. As the name suggests, oysters are the attraction here; The Solo Diner's never been a fan of bivalves, so he sticks with Pearl's perfectly prepared but pricey whole fish (served à la carte; sides are extra). A good West Village alternative the tourists haven't discovered yet.

Penang
109 Spring Street (between Greene and Mercer)
212-274-8883

64 Third Avenue (at 11th Street)
212-228-7888

Imagine Trader Vic's—and all that tiki-tacky decor—reincarnated with not quite authentic but quite tasty Malaysian food, and you have Penang. There really is no other way to describe a place that serves mango ice cream with a paper umbrella. The staff is as likely to be blond/blue-eyed Europeans wearing sarongs over their south-of-14th-Street basic black clothes as Asian. Still, for the timid, Penang is a good introduction to Malaysian cuisine. Try the beef rendang. The list of wine by the glass is limited, but includes the pleasant surprise of a sangiovese blend. The Third Avenue Penang has an active if amusing bar scene, but the back dining rooms are quiet and pleasant, with just enough light to read by.

Petite Abeille

400 West 14th Street (at Ninth Avenue)
212-727-1505

466 Hudson Street (at Barrow Street)
212-741-6479
$ $
See page 17.

Pink Teacup

42 Grove Street (between Bedford and Bleecker)
212-807-6755

Blink and you might miss it; this microscopic West Village institution has been dishing out authentic soul food since 1954. The atmosphere is overstuffed Southern living room. About half the tables here are two-tops, so solo diners get the same down-home treatment as couples and groups (packed weekend brunch hours, however, are dicier). The only drawback is iffy lighting in the evening. If you're here, you've already given up on watching cholesterol and/or calories for the duration of your meal, so dive in; the fried chicken, salmon croquettes, catfish with black-eyed peas and collard greens, and corn fritters are pure temptation. If you can bear it, save room for dessert. Every one is homemade, and the sweet potato pie is euphoria. Breakfast here is also famous, with heavenly biscuits and grits among the offerings; lunch specials are a pittance at $6.25. P.S. If you forget reading material, you can pass the moments perusing the autographed photos of celebrity customers (Oprah, Denzel, and so forth) lining the walls. Bring your own alcohol.

Pizzeria Uno Chicago
391 Avenue of the Americas (between 8th Street and Waverly Place)
212-242-5230

55 Third Avenue (between 10th and 11th Streets)
212-995-9668
See page 18.

Quintessence
263 East 10th Street (between First Avenue and Avenue A)
646-654-1823

$ $ ⑂ ⑂ ⑂

🧑 🧑 🧑 🧑

♟ ♟ ♟ ♟   🛋 🛋 🛋 🛋

Ya gotta have a gimmick, and does this place ever: cuisine
here is "a hundred percent raw . . . uncooked, unpasteur-
ized, and unprocessed," according to a menu/manifesto.
The concept works more often than it should; a killer gua-
camole, tasty wild rice salad with avocado and mango, and
spaghetti-like squash in marinara sauce are just plain delicious, cooked or not. Unfortunately, dishes like nut loaf
("nutmeat" with spices, veggies, and gravy) and "livioli" (a
sort of vegetarian ravioli) are, to be polite, an acquired
taste. But solo diners will love the bright, soothing room in
subtle shades of lime, the warm and patient service (waiters and waitresses here get a lot of questions), and the irresistible desserts, like a healthful pecan pie, coconut cream
pie "packed with electrolytes," and fruit fondue. Good
lighting, even at night. P.S. All combos on the bargain $10
lunch menu come with "young coconut juice."

Savoy

70 Prince Street (at Crosby Street)

212-219-8570

$ $ $ ⑂ ⑂ ⑂ ⑂ ⑂

🧑 🧑 🧑 🧑   Y Y Y Y

♟ ♟ ♟   🛋 🛋 🛋 🛋 🛋

Now that Savoy has graduated from scene restaurant to
neighborhood standby, it's safe for solo diners to enjoy
alongside the crowds. At peak hours, mind you, both the
pretty upstairs and downstairs rooms still get claustrophobic, but The Solo Diner has enjoyed lunches and dinners
here where the staff acted like he was the only one in the

room. (P.S. He prefers sitting downstairs, by the window, or on the adjacent banquette opposite the Prince Street windows.) The menu boasts imaginative uses of vegetable purees and sides with fish and game entrées. Well-chosen wine list too, with strong selections by the glass. A working fireplace downstairs warms diners in winter months. Remember to reserve here; avoid weekends.

Second Avenue Deli

156 Second Avenue (at 10th Street)

212-677-0606

$ $ 🍴 🍴 🍴 🍴

🪑 🪑   🍸 🍸

🛎 🛎 🛎 🛎   🪑 🪑 🪑 🪑

Single diners are always welcome here, but no one lingers. You come, you nosh, you go. In any case, it remains the most authentic of New York's big three delis. The Solo Diner knows someone in California who visits New York frequently. When it comes time for him to return, he has the taxi take him to the airport by way of the Second Avenue Deli to pick up some pastrami to take back to the West Coast. Not that he'd spurn the chopped liver or the matzoh ball soup. The Second Avenue Deli inspires that sort of passionate loyalty, although its main stock in trade these days seems to be nostalgia for the good old days of Jewish-American culture.

Souen East

28 East 13th Street (at University Place and
Fifth Avenue)

212-627-7150

Souen West

210 Sixth Avenue (at Prince Street)

212-807-7421

$ $

With their inviting, open layouts, warm service, and delicious macrobiotic cooking, these places have attracted loyal followings among healthy foodies. For solo diners, Souen is a particular treat. Both locations boast a number of comfortable small tables that are nearly always occupied by singles, and lighting is terrific in both as well. The Solo Diner has never had a disappointing experience with the food here. If you're looking for the standard plates of vegetables and grains, Souen has those, but more adventuresome palates will be rewarded with specials like a delicious mash of yams, onions, and carrots; sesame-seed-crusted tuna steak, perfectly cooked; hearty soups like black bean; and a thick Japanese broth loaded with vegetables and tofu. Desserts—all nondairy—are delicious as well. Weekend brunch, with organic waffles, pancakes, oatmeal, and tofu scrambles, is a must. Fine selection of surprisingly good organic wines by the glass. P.S. The 13th Street location, near Union Square, is a bilevel space with a peaceful upstairs seating area.

Spring Street Natural

62 Spring Street (at Lafayette Street)

212-966-0290

$

The Solo Diner goes hot and cold about Spring Street Natural. It's one of the older vegetarian restaurants below 14th Street—indeed, below Houston—and has always had a relaxed, tranquil atmosphere. There's more space than is usual between tables in Manhattan restaurants, and they're larger than usual. The food is organic and carefully prepared with interesting seasonings that can often make the "seeds and weeds" matter. Alas, the lighting is a bit too dim for older eyes to read by, and the service can be even more relaxed than the atmosphere, making things less than tranquil. Instead, focus on your plate. A Mediterranean salad, with feta, roasted peppers, and onions, is generous and vibrant; grilled fish dishes are well-prepared, with inviting side dishes like yams or sugar snap peas; stir-fries are delicious. Yes, wines can be organic; no, you don't go to a natural foods restaurant for the wine list.

St. Dymphna's

118 St. Mark's Place (between First Avenue and Avenue A)

212-254-6636

$ $

Depending upon whom you ask, St. Dymphna is the patron saint of mental health or of the insane. You might be driven to the latter by the eccentric service at this Irish pub-cum-restaurant, which also happens to have excellent food and a lovely garden to eat in during good weather. But it's welcoming of solos and popular with locals who like to linger in the literate laid-back Irish charm. While it's not the sort of place to bother you if you wanted to linger to finish a book, it might be a bit dark for older eyes. The hearty Irish breakfasts here are highly recommended; they're served with a lovely brunch menu until five P.M. on weekends.

Taste of Tokyo
54 West 13th Street (between Fifth and Sixth Avenues)
212-691-8666
$ $

This is one of The Solo Diner's favorite places. It's also one of the cooler sushi spots in New York, with anything from techno to Joni Mitchell on the stereo and a boisterous staff. He comes back so often not only for the luscious, well-priced fish, but because the waiters have doted on him since the day he started coming. Be warned: it gets extraordinarily loud in here, and most of the clientele seem to schedule their important phone calls for the moments between the appetizer and main course. On warm evenings you'll also have to cool your heels outside; a line is inevitable.

Tavern on Jane
31 Jane Street (at Eighth Avenue)
212-675-2526
$ $

If you didn't know Tavern on Jane was there, you'd probably pass it by—and most of the regulars probably wouldn't mind. But once you find it, you'll be glad you did. Quiet, solid, and dependable as a great neighborhood restaurant should be, Tavern on Jane treats solo diners like friends;

you'll see at least one or two fellow travelers in the darkish but comfy dining room on any given night. Once settled in, pay close attention to the specials, which are usually winners. The regular menu's alluring too, with updated comfort food like roast chicken with garlic mashed potatoes, mixed green salad with marinated, grilled steak, and pastas. You'll feel comfortable lingering here for a while, so leave room for dessert.

Telephone Bar & Grill
149 Second Avenue (between 9th and 10th Streets)
212-529-5000
$ $

There are four red Dr. Who telephone booths in the facade of Telephone. The brick-lined interior has various telephone-related signs mixed in with the usual pseudo-British pub regalia. Tables are cramped together, which is why The Solo Diner's favorite table is in what most would consider an undesirable spot: near the waiters' station. The place can be noisy—there is a discreet bar scene—and the lights are low. The usual pub standards are here—fish and chips, shepherd's pie—as well as a more varied and interesting menu of daily specials. Only four or five wines are offered by the glass, but the selection changes periodically and often includes imaginative selections such as a Viognier.

Thali
28 Greenwich Avenue (between Seventh Avenue South and Charles Street)
212-367-7411

A sliver of a restaurant—there are only eight tables—this unself-consciously hip West Village Indian place specializes in set meals known as thali. They're an array of small portions presented on a metal serving plate, including favorites like lentils, basmati rice, spinach and cheese, and they're all very good. Thalis are also an ideal meal for one (The Solo Diner practically lived on these on his trip through India). Only one waitperson is usually on duty here at any given time, and they welcome solo diners with enthusiasm, probably for companionship. Set plates are just $6 at lunch and $10 at dinner, so for diners on a budget this is a find. No alcohol is served, but you can bring your own.

Thé Adoré

17 East 13th Street (between Fifth Avenue and University Place)

212-243-7411

What do you mean, you've never been to a French sandwicherie and pastry shop run by stylish Japanese twenty-somethings? Of course, New York has one, and lucky for us, it's ideal for snacking solo with a good read in hand (hours are limited to breakfast and lunch). The salads and sandwiches here are meticulously prepared, the coffee's strong and delicious, and the bright upstairs dining room is ultraminimal but relaxing. If you're in the neighborhood, treat yourself.

Celebrity Sound Bite

I dine solo a lot, not just because I can't get anyone to go with me, but because I love the freedom of being able to eat where I want and when I want, and also to be able to leave when I choose. Being an only child with a vivid inner life, I've always been comfortable going solo, and in fact cherish the opportunity to spend quality time with myself.

In Padella (145 Second Avenue at 9th Street; 212-598-9800) is one of my favorite places at which to do this. It's not overly trendy or filled with people wondering why you're alone. In fact, no one really cares—plus, the service is personable and the food's reasonable and delicious. I might take myself there really soon if I'm not busy.

—Michael Musto

Village Voice columnist, author, and television personality

Tibet on Houston
136 West Houston Street
212-995-5884
$ $

It was the sight of a Himalayan woman carrying a small child in a traditional sling that caught The Solo Diner's attention and led to finding Tibet on Houston. Go down a flight of steps and you might as well have climbed up the Himalayas: inside, it's serene, with Buddhas on one wall and prayer flags on the other. The momos are good, but there are other Tibetan specialties here, all well-prepared: a fried curried chicken (jhasha khatsa), say, or spicy spare ribs. In good weather a few tables are put out front, but The Solo Diner prefers to be inside away from the noise and traffic along Houston Street. Solo diners are treated respectfully here.

Village Natural

123 Greenwich Avenue (between Seventh Avenue South and Charles Street)

212-727-0968

$

Since this serene West Village stalwart never really gets crowded—The Solo Diner can't figure out why—a table for one can often mean a spacious booth or a big round table (a favorite is the one opposite the cash register). The room is bright even though it's down a half flight of stairs, the noise level's low, and the food several notches above most "natural" food places. Servers are mostly amateurs, but eager to please and mostly charming in their attempts. Try to regard them as part of the experience and concentrate on savoring a thick, dairy-free corn chowder soup that should win prizes, simple fish preparations, heaping plates of steamed vegetables and grains, and standbys like hummus or nondairy burritos.

Yaffa Café

97 St. Mark's Place (between First Avenue and Avenue A)
212-674-9302

$ 🍴 🍴 🍴

Along with Dojo (see page 35), this is one of the reigning East Village cheap-chic establishments. It's open seven days a week, twenty-four hours a day, and solo diners seem present throughout. They come for the massive salads, heaping stir-fries, and simple chicken dishes; they usually come back for the boho vibe, edgy-but-friendly service, and an environment where they know they'll be left alone with their thoughts, reading material, or whatever else they walked in with. Lighting is good during the day, adequate at night. Decor is a charming, well-conceived mess. Beware weekend brunches, when slumming uptown hordes descend.

14TH STREET TO 42ND STREET

Union Square, Gramercy Park, Chelsea, Murray Hill, Midtown South

ONCE UPON A time, Midtown South had lots of department stores in and around Murray Hill and Penn Station. The Solo Diner not only could eat at any one of those emporia, but also at a large number of restaurants specializing in feeding the ladies who lunch—alone or in packs. There was the Charleston Garden on the eighth floor of B. Altman's & Co., which was, for a generation of New Yorkers, the world's best-loved bad restaurant; and Mary Elizabeth, an eccentric tearoom that exiled men to the back of the establishment.

Nowadays, you have fashionable dining in the Flatiron district and in Chelsea. Murray Hill, less residential than it once was, now caters to a business crowd, while Rosehill—the area around Gramercy Park that's not Gramercy Park—remains local and residential and more often than not amiable to solo diners. Little Korea—32nd Street, near Penn Station—is a two-block row of Korean restaurants that will satisfy your single-dining needs and kimchee jones. Chelsea, because it is the new "Gay Ghetto," is much more accepting of diners—indeed anyone—who doesn't fit pre-conceived notions, for obvious reasons. It's also the sort of place where, if you're a friendly solo diner, you'll find a friendly waiter.

Alley's End

311 West 17th Street (between Eighth and Ninth Avenues)
212-627-8899

$ $

Everybody's best-kept secret, Alley's End is tucked away down a flight of stairs in a notch off West 17th Street. A sort of midscale place with upscale aspirations, it largely succeeds; service is solicitous, the newish-American food is well-executed, and the dark, low-key decor (including a little babbling brook) succeeds at making you forget you're in Manhattan. Best of all, Alley's End has warmly welcomed The Solo Diner on nights when he never even expected to get a table. From the smiling hostess to the friendly servers, he was made to feel completely at home here, not an easy task in a buzzing room in Chelsea. Fish dishes are stand-outs, as are the signature homemade sausages, which change daily; appetizers are overpriced and usually skippable.

Amy's Bread

75 Ninth Avenue (in Chelsea Market, at 15th Street)
212-462-4338

$

For some, Amy's Bread has the best bread in the city. It also offers interesting sandwiches, such as the crowd-pleasing Tuscan: two kinds of salami, prosciutto, provolone, and tomato. Although it's more for lunch on the run, it's highly recommended as an alternative to West Chelsea's high-priced scene restaurants. Cash only. P.S. You can walk off your sandwich in the cool, cavernous Chelsea Market, twenty food-related wholesale and retail businesses opened in 1997 in a renovated complex built between 1880 and 1930, anchored by what was once the original Nabisco Oreo Cookie factory.

Antique Café
101 West 25th Street (at Sixth Avenue)
212-675-1663
$ 🍴 🍴 🍴 🍴
👤 👤 👤
🪑 🪑 🪑 🪑 🪑   🏛 🏛 🏛 🏛 🏛

Blink and you might miss this tiny, homey takeaway joint with eight small tables and a counter loaded with delicious sandwiches, salads, and desserts. You'll always find solo diners here, some from nearby offices, some (on weekends) taking a break from the flea market across the street that gives this place its name. The counter service is ditzy but friendly; The Solo Diner frequently has to interrupt telephone conversations to get attention from the staff. Try the bulging tuna sandwich (with only a *hint* of mayonnaise, the dieting Solo Diner was assured), quiches, rosemary roasted chicken, lemon cake, and fudge cookies (which sabotaged the diet). Since there's not much else around on this emerging strip of Sixth Avenue, this place is especially welcome. Lighting is terrific.

Bachué

36 West 21st Street (between Fifth and Sixth Avenues)
212-229-0870

$ ♥ ♥ ♥ ♥

👤 👤 👤 👤

🍴 🍴 🍴 🍴 🍴   ᏛᏛᏛᏛᏛ

Bachué, instructs the menu, is named after "the beautiful goddess of Colombia's Chibcha people." This compact Flatiron-area vegetarian does her proud with a small but wide-ranging menu of fresh, healthful specialties. Bachué also smiles on solo diners; almost every table here is a two-top, and the lighting is ideal for reading at all hours. Starters might include a refreshing salad of sea vegetables and lettuce, creamy hummus with pita bread, or cold soba noodles with peanut sauce, almost a meal in itself. All of the entrees are delicious, from a burrito made with seitan, tempeh, or tofu to Japanese nori rolls to well-prepared pastas. Fresh juices are an invigorating accompaniment. The staff is sincere and warm, if a bit overworked. Busiest at lunchtime, when it fills up with workers from surrounding offices on this commercial block. P.S. Breakfast is served until three P.M., including unbeatable porridge with fruit and a knockout Latin traditional breakfast with beans, rice, plantains, tortillas, soup, slaw, and salsa.

Back Porch

488 Third Avenue (at 33rd Street)
212-685-3828

$ ♥ ♥ ♥

👤 👤 👤 👤   🍸 🍸

🍴 🍴 🍴   ᏛᏛᏛ

Strictly speaking, the Back Porch falls somewhere in between a sports bar and a singles bar. In reality, it's a comfortable place for a business or social lunch, with a pleasant staff and a varied if light menu. The bar is usually busy, but it's more grain than grape. Wines by the glass are not only predictable, but also mediocre. Food is good, however, and often serves up New York twists on traditional regional dishes, like the quesadilla with lox and cream cheese. Because the Back Porch is near where The Solo Diner works, he has dealt with this place for requests for tables ranging from one to eleven and has always been accommodated. But his favorite moment came one balmy evening when there seemed to be few customers on the outside dining area. The host came up to him and made an offer: a lovely table outside with minimal service or a table inside with normal service.

Bendix Diner

219 Eighth Avenue (at 21st Street)
212-366-0560
$

Only in New York: Bendix Diner is owned by a friendly Israeli and his Thai wife, who serve up a mean Pad Thai and stir-fries along with hearty meat loaf and tasty breakfast fare. In Chelsea, a hub of social dining, this place is a solo-dining refuge. It's not fancy, and the cooking sometimes misses the mark, but singles are always welcome, and there's a row of small tables against the window facing Eighth Avenue. Prices are very reasonable. P.S. Bendix Diner's motto is "Get Fat!"

This is ironic, considering the staggering number of buff gym bodies on parade around here.

Blockhead's Burritos
499 Third Avenue (between 33rd and 34th Streets)
212-213-3332
$

New York boasts countless Mexican joints, but Blockhead's deserves a special mention. Cheap, clever, and well-run, it offers some unusual Mexican-inspired creations along with the familiar burritos, quesadillas, and fajitas. There's a vegetable burrito for herbivores, a nondairy version, and wackier renditions like tangy Carolina BBQ or jerk chicken. Good wraps, sandwiches, and salads round out the inexpensive menu. Since they're used to constant traffic from nearby office workers tired of deli salad bars, the servers are accustomed to accommodating tables for one. The only downside here is the crowd, which starts forming around 11:30 and doesn't abate until well after three P.M. Lighting is excellent, and while it's far from fancy, the atmosphere is upbeat, enjoyable, and real.

Bright Food Shop
216 Eighth Avenue (between 21st and 22nd Streets)
212-243-4433
$ $

By keeping most of its original interiors, this former greasy spoon has become a haven for solo diners in Chelsea. Com-

Celebrity Sound Bite

I usually go to one of three places on the Upper West Side when I dine/snack alone. EJ's Luncheonette (432 Avenue of the Americas; 212-473-5555) when it's not too busy in the midafternoon. They don't rush me out, the food is simple, and I can read comfortably and not get bothered. Columbus Bakery (957 First Avenue; 212-421-0034), which is seat-yourself and crowded most middays, and I am always there for breakfast on Saturdays and Sundays to read the papers. And Bruculino's (225 Columbus Avenue; 212-579-3966) restaurant on Columbus, a family restaurant that does a good business. Occasionally I will drop by there late for dinner after work. The staff is oh-so-attentive that even when I am alone, I am not, because the hostess or waitresses always come over to chat, and actually have sat down with me. I'm a simple kinda guy . . .

—Jeff Simmons
Investigative Reporter
NY1 News

pact and brightly lit—with a nifty neon sign outside—it features a long and comfortable counter, ideally lit for reading. The Solo Diner enjoys it more than the tables (though those are readily available). Bright Food Shop is super-casual, and the crowd's so cool no one will pretend to be interested in what you're eating or reading. You may find it hard not to stare at other diners' plates, though; the kitchen here turns out highly original Latin/Asian fusion dishes that blow away many restaurants that charge double for less creative fare. The menu changes often, but if you can catch them, don't miss the moo-shu burritos, spicy soba noodles with greens, and seared salmon. The formerly dry restaurant also offers a very limited beer and wine selection, including a couple of selections by the glass.

Café 18
8 East 18th Street (between 5th Avenue and Broadway)
212-620-4182
$ 🍴🍴🍴🍴
👤 👤
🏮 🏮 🏮 🏮 🏮   🏮 🏮 🏮 🏮 🏮

The Solo Diner remembers a frightening meal at a now-defunct Garment District kosher restaurant that nearly made him renounce his faith. Luckily, the "cholov yisroel" (dairy), strictly kosher offerings at this loftlike café have restored it. All chicken and turkey dishes here use soy substitutes, but The Solo Diner prefers the straight-on meat-free dishes anyway. A tasty salmon burger, Salad Niçoise, delicious sweet carrot salad, and hefty stuffed acorn squash all stand as shining examples of quality, casual kosher. There's much more on the menu, which ranges from burritos to lasagna. The space itself is ideally designed for solo dining; a rack of newspapers greets you at the door, and there are plenty of tables in the expansive, well-lighted room. It's never been crowded on any of The Solo Diner's visits, so there is always an abundance of servers working the floor (more often than not discussing career plans or interpersonal issues, which makes for compelling eaves-dropping). No alcohol served.

The City Bakery
3 West 18th Street (between Fifth Avenue and Avenue of the Americas)
212-366-1414

$ 🍴🍴🍴🍴

👤 👤 👤

🪑 🪑 🪑 🪑 🪑   🎴 🎴 🎴 🎴 🎴

This popular-with-locals place really did start out as a bakery, back when the Flatiron/lower Fifth Avenue neighborhood wasn't so hot. Over the years, City Bakery's added a self-serve lunch with some of the area's best market-fresh offerings—and prices to match. The Solo Diner loves the grilled veggies, sliced breast of chicken, and salads. Breakfast, of course, is still a staple, with gigantic muffins, scones, and baked goods, and tremendous coffee. The industrial-chic space houses many small tables; they're perfect for solo diners. Perfect lighting too. P.S. It's mandatory to try one of the cakes or pastries here!

City Chow Cafe (at Equinox Fitness Club)
895 Broadway (at 19th Street)
212-780-9300

$ 🍴🍴🍴🍴

👤 👤 👤

🪑 🪑 🪑 🪑 🪑   🎴 🎴 🎴 🎴 🎴

Dining solo in a gym sounds as much fun as a root canal. But Equinox isn't an ordinary gym—"Sex and the City" films here frequently—and City Chow Cafe, its slick snack bar, offers cheap, healthful fare in a groovy setting (the buff trainers and clients lounging around aren't bad either). Not just for members, City Chow Cafe has become an active solo-diner scene. Since most of the clubs open early and close very late, the cafés make an appealing choice for a quick breakfast, lunch, or light dinner. All locations serve the same rotating menu; you'll usually find a daily soup (corn chowder and minestrone make regular appearances), generous salads like mesclun greens with grilled chicken, fruit concoctions, and solid sandwiches prepared without a lot of junk.

City Crab & Seafood Co.

235 Park Avenue South (at 19th Street)
212-529-3800
$ $

This is where The Solo Diner goes to feed his crab jones (alert readers will notice how many times crab is mentioned in these reviews). As the name suggests, crab is the specialty here: hard shell, soft shell, king, Dungeness, and more, done up as crab soup, crab cakes, and crab salad, among other preparations. After crabs, the raw bar is best. For the rest of the menu, the simpler the preparation, the better the selection is likely to be. Wines by the glass are limited, but a little more interesting than usual. The Solo Diner can't remember the last time a Riesling was part of such a list. The decor is rustic Maryland crab house—nautical and fishing motifs down to various shellfish traps and oversize model crabs. Downstairs can be quite noisy, but the balcony and mezzanine are quieter, if not quiet. Singles tend to be seated downstairs at high tables for five. The host or hostess can easily be persuaded to seat aces upstairs.

Cosi/Xando

3 East 17th Street (between Fifth Avenue and Broadway)
212-414-8468

11 West 42nd Street (between Fifth and Sixth Avenues)
212-398-6660
See page 9.

The Cottage

33 Irving Place (at 16th Street)
212-505-8600

$

There are many Chinese restaurants in New York. The Solo Diner chose not to include most of them in this book, since most serve similar food in drearily identical settings. He's making an exception for The Cottage, which almost seems like it was designed with solo diners in mind. The room is bright, open, high-ceilinged, and modern; the welcome has never been less than warm, even at peak hours; and the prime tables against the huge windows facing Irving Place are all two-tops, where the hostess never hesitates to seat a single. The food is very good, and relatively clean and light for this kind of fare; The Solo Diner usually sticks with steamed chicken and vegetables and has sampled a respectable shredded beef Szechuan style and calamari in black bean sauce. The only thing The Cottage shares with more mundane Chinese establishments is the dull house wines by the glass.

Eisenberg Sandwich Shop

174 Fifth Avenue (between 22nd and 23rd Streets)

212-675-5096

$

Don't let the gruff counter staff scare you at this old-fashioned Flatiron favorite; they may tease about what you ordered or how you ordered it, but it's all part of the routine among servers who've been here since velociraptors roamed Fifth Avenue. Usually packed with solo diners along its slightly greasy counter and five tables, Eisenberg's serves what's rumored to be New York's best tuna fish sandwich, along with basics like meat loaf, matzoh ball soup, and turkey sandwiches. It may be a squeeze to read as you eat at the counter, but it's worth it for the experience.

El Quijote

226 West 23rd Street (between Seventh and Eighth Avenues)

212-929-1855

$ $

Adventuresome solo diners, take note: El Quijote is one of several establishments in the ground floor of the Chelsea Hotel. It's right in line with a shop selling musical instruments, a comic book store, and a tattoo parlor. You go in, hoping that it will turn out to be more shabby than seedy, which is just about right. This very literal Spanish restaurant has been around for some sixty years, and the decor screams midcentury Hispanophile, à la Frank Sinatra and Ava Gardner. Lobster specials and paella are the thing here, and there is no other reason to go. Though the food could use some improvement, tables for one are as welcome as tables for four or six. Service manages to be professional and sullen at the same time. The bartenders are old-time pros and may make conversation while they mix you perfect drinks.

Eleven Madison Park

11 Madison Avenue (at 25th Street)

212-889-0905

$ $ $ $

Part of the Danny Meyer mini-empire of New York casual-luxury restaurants, including Gramercy Tavern and Union Square Café, all of which are renowned for being single-friendly. The Solo Diner might best describe this restaurant as not single-unfriendly. There are some three dozen wines by the glass. There is also the soaring art deco interior that overlooks Madison Park (once Madison Square, and the original location of Madison Square Garden), and a kitchen that presents a new American cuisine homage to the old-fashioned "continental" cuisine that used to be Eleven Madison's bill of fare. The result is at times more interesting than successful, but recommended dishes include lobster pot au feu and a plate of lemon desserts.

F&B

269 West 23rd Street (between Seventh and Eighth Avenues)

646-486-4441

$

It stands for Frites & Beignets, in case you're wondering. And that's what you'll find here, along with elaborately dressed hot dogs and even Swedish meatballs. They're served in a narrow, minimalist space, with a soothing glow from the blue-washed walls. F&B has no tables, but solo diners will be happy with the bar stools along dining counters on either side of the space. It's a cheerful departure from most Chelsea restaurants, which lately seem to have been cut from the same expensive cloth. Put that diet on hold and dig into the Great Dane (Danish hot dog with remoulade, roasted onions, marinated cucumber), sweet potato frites, or a beignet dipped in chocolate, honey, or crème anglaise. Beer, cider, wine, and champagne are available, including a surprisingly generous selection of wines by the glass. P.S. Many selections here are available with vegetarian hot dogs.

Follonico
6 West 24th Street (between Fifth and Sixth Avenues)
212-691-6359
$ $ $

Follonico has lousy service—spacey, slow, and slack. Still, if you can shore up some patience and pretend you're dining in a Tuscan farmhouse at a leisurely pace, there are pleasures to be savored here for solo diners. The small, subdued room, a favorite of local publishing honchos, is painted in warm earth tones, with a wood-burning brick oven in the back. It feels cozy in winter, oasislike in summer. There are a number of tables for one, including a couple you can't see from the entrance, in a corner to the extreme right of the maitre d's station. The lighting throughout is very comfortable, and the vibe subdued enough that solo diners won't feel out of place—a rarity in the happening Flatiron district. Menus change frequently, but recent offerings have included endive, artichoke, and fava beans, and wood-roasted calamari appetizers, as well as succulent rabbit, whole roasted fish in a rock salt crust, and a perfectly turned-out rack of lamb. The Solo Diner has always been able to secure a table for one without trouble. Unfortunately, Follonico loses major points for a wine list that includes only one selection by the glass at lunch, and just a couple more at dinner.

Gramercy Tavern

123 East 20th Street (between Broadway and Park Avenue South)

212-477-0777

$ $ $ $ 🍴 🍴 🍴 🍴

🖊   🍷 🍷 🍷

🪑 🪑 🪑 🪑   🛎 🛎 🛎

Another in Danny Meyer's mini-empire of restaurants (see Eleven Madison Park), Gramercy Tavern stumbles. With the more formal (and expensive) dining room in the back, the front bar at this clubby restaurant doubles as a café. On repeated visits, The Solo Diner was ignored by service staff, despite pleading looks for basics like water and a fresh napkin; obtaining the check required sophisticated psychological warfare. Even worse, overflow from the packed bar made evening meals loud and claustrophobic. A shame, because a faux-homey ambience, comfortable tables, and ample lighting would make this an ideal choice when The

Solo Diner feels like splurging. Food is upscale simple; filet mignon arrived pink inside and perfectly cooked; halibut was firm and buttery-tasting; desserts were straightforward and delicious. Think strategically if you want to chance it.

Hangawi

12 West 32nd Street (between Fifth and Madison)
212-213-0077

$ $ $

Hangawi may be New York's most exotic dining experience. For the duration of a meal, you are transported into an elegant and serene Zen Buddhist monastery, somewhere in the mountains of Korea. You take off your shoes, sit at a low table, and eat all sorts of vegetarian delights while calming otherworldly music plays quietly in the background. And then there's the milky-white rice wine . . . The staff moves so gracefully . . . Or is that just your mind waving? Despite the ethereal atmosphere, the lighting is just right for reading, if you can focus . . .

I Trulli

122 East 27th Street (between Park and Lexington)
212-481-7372

$ $ $

I Trulli specializes in the cuisine from Apulia, which is in the heel of Italy (The Solo Diner cheated and looked it up). The food here is hearty and rustic: lusty braised rabbit, rich medallions of wild boar, refined grilled mackerel with eggplant. Service is smooth and professional in an atmosphere of urban sophistication; lots of neighborhood advertising and media types seem to make this a second home. The fireplace is enclosed in glass, and a glass wall faces a garden where you can dine, weather permitting. A caveat: a hostess here did get snippy when The Solo Diner turned up without a reservation. P.S. The ambience in here can get romantic at night, so if that's a turnoff, look elsewhere. Small but well-selected list of wines by the glass, including what must be the only Apulian wine in the tristate area.

Jackson Hole Burgers
521 Third Avenue (at 35th Street)
212-679-3264
See page 132.

La Lunchonette
130 Tenth Avenue (at 18th Street)
212-675-0342

$ $

As West Chelsea's become white-hot, restaurants have followed. But La Lunchonette beat the trendies by several years. This beloved spot opened when the neighborhood was barely a neighborhood and the surrounding galleries and clubs were still warehouses. It's a wonderful choice for a table for one; the full menu of light French standards is served at the bar, where you can join a colorful cast of regulars. Or grab one of the well-lighted tables for two along the wall near the entrance (though your chances decrease after eight P.M.). Daily specials are the way to order, with cleaned-up classic preparations of fish, beef, and pork. Desserts and coffee are routine, though.

Le Café Creme
165 Madison Avenue (at 33rd Street)
212-679-8077

$ $

Café Creme is basically a lunch place, although there is an evening prix fixe. The small well-lighted room is often filled at midday, including some tables for one. This is also a place where women feel comfortable. On most days, there are more women lunching here than men. Café Creme serves light, not nouvelle, French food: omelettes, salads, quiche. All quite good, as are such more serious offerings as cold salmon in green sauce. The staff is friendly and professional, although they can get harried during peak hours, which is when English is most likely to desert the francophone staff.

Le Gamin
183 Ninth Avenue (at 21st Street)
212-243-8864
See page 46.

Lemon
230 Park Avenue South (between 18th and 19th Streets)
212-614-1200

$ $

Lemon is not a lemon. You'll get moderately good food that's moderately overpriced. The service is moderately friendly and moderately professional. It looks quite alluring for solo diners since there's a magazine stand of sorts in the front. And The Solo Diner did find the tiny tables in front with the old firehouse doors open to the street a delightful place to sit, read, and watch Park Avenue South's glamour industry and wannabe types walk by. On a second visit, on a midweek night, a hostess was quite willing to seat The Solo Diner in a booth for four despite arriving around seven P.M. Menu is dressed-up salads, pastas, and fish, dubbed "progressive American" here.

Lemongrass Grill

138 East 34th Street

212-213-3317

See page 12.

L'Express

249 Park Avenue South (at 20th Street)

212-254-5858

$ $

This mini-chain of what New Yorkers imagine a French bistro to be like is open twenty-four hours a day. And that's its main draw. Because of its schedule, it's clear the servers at this place have seen it all, and they don't bat an eye at requests for a table for one. Solo diners get the same treatment of benign neglect as do tables for two or four. Focus on your reading material and enjoy the surroundings. One friend has described L'Express as the best French restaurant in New York—at three A.M. To be fair, the food is improving.

Live Bait

14 East 23rd Street (between Fifth and Madison)

212-353-2400

$ $

Truth be told, all restaurants in New York are pretentious to a greater or lesser extent. In the case of Live Bait, the pretensions are that it's a Southern redneck white-trash dive of a bar. Well, it is a bar, and the food does reflect the restaurant's pretensions. The twist here is that the food is pretty good and the restaurant is more solo diner tolerant than most of its ilk. The downside is the noise level and the bar scene—hormonal frat boys chasing after live bait . . . er, young ladies with the come-hither in the eye—is depressing to anyone over thirty-five.

Mayrose

920 Broadway (at 21st Street)

212-533-3663

$

Since this place is in The Solo Diner's neighborhood, he's been a regular from the day it opened. And for good reason: the light, airy interior, abundance of small tables, basket of newspapers on the counter, and chatty servers make it one of the area's most welcoming spots for a table for one. A sort of nouveau diner with a sense of humor (chicken soup is called "penicillin" on the menu), Mayrose turns out terrific omelettes, sandwiches, salads, even matzoh brei, at fair prices. On those weekend mornings when the line spills out the door, a seat at the comfortable counter isn't a bad alternative. Best for breakfast and lunch. P.S. Solo diners can amuse themselves by eavesdropping as tourists struggle to pronounce "challah" (as in "challah French toast").

Mumbles
179 Third Avenue (at 17th Street)
212-477-6066

Mumbles Restaurant & Bar
603 Second Avenue (between 33rd and 34th Streets)
212-889-0750

$ $

Is it a table for one if it's a solo diner and the solo diner's dog? This is a favorite with Chico, the canine in question, and his solo-dining owner, during the summer when outdoor seating at the Third Avenue branch becomes a watering hole for solo diners and their dogs. As for the inside: surprisingly, these seventies-swingers-vibe restaurant/bars turned out to be quite welcoming and especially comfortable for solo diners, even inside and without dogs. The food's inexpensive and good, with the many daily specials a highlight: pastas, fish, and soups are all solid bets. Lighting's good, in spite of the bar atmosphere. You'll see many fellow travelers here on any given night.

Park Bistro
414 Park Avenue South (between 28th and 29th Streets)
212-689-1360

$ $ $

Park Bistro is one of few authentic French restaurants left in New York that has the integrity of its pretensions. The decor is locked into postwar Paris: dark red banquettes and framed French film posters. The waiters wear white aprons. The food is well-above-average bistro fare. Singles are served with professionalism, if not always warmth, so off hours are probably a better choice. On the other hand, The Solo Diner once turned up during a torrential rainstorm, a bedraggled sight that brought out a waiter's inner grand-mère. Lunch is a business scene.

Petite Abeille
107 West 18th Street (between Sixth and Seventh Avenues)
212-604-9350
See page 17.

Pipa
888 Broadway (ABC Carpet & Home at 19th Street)
212-677-2233

$ $ $

Pipa is one of two restaurants celebrity chef Douglas Rodriguez created for ABC Carpet & Home. From the culinary point of view, that would be reason enough for a visit. But because of the nature of tapas, it is almost de rigueur for a solo diner. Tapas are small appetizer portions of fish or meat, vegetables, or bread. You order as many or as few as you want. Because the portions tend not to be even as big as an appetizer, a solo diner can happily sample all sorts of dishes he or she might have to skip ordinarily. The decor falls somewhere between a Himalayan bordello a bit south of Shangri-La and a Gypsy encampment in Andalusia. Service can be eccentric, but is usually prompt. The wine list is better than average, though The Solo Diner would have favored even more emphasis on Spanish and/or South American wines. Food is not quite as interesting as the nuevo Latino cuisine for which Rodriguez is known and that he created for Patria and Chicama. The limits of working within a purely Spanish tradition seems to hamper him. Nevertheless, it's still among the best in town.

Republic

37 Union Square West (at 17th Street)

212-627-7172

$

If the quality of the food here matched the perfection of the setting, this place could be a solo diner's nirvana. Republic's hallmark is its communal seating, but the hosts/hostesses often discourage solo diners from those; The Solo Diner much prefers the counter anyway. A long stone bar with comfortable stools and perfect lighting complements the smart, sparse, sleek design of both cavernous restaurants. Service is brisk but friendly and highly efficient, with beautiful servers of all genders more attentive than you'd expect. But the famed noodle dishes vary in quality; aside from a superb Pad Thai, the specialty noodle dishes here range from mediocre to inedible, and often arrive cold or congealed. Stick with the basics and avoid dishes with meat (The Solo Diner's nicknamed one of them "chicken tetrachloride"). Worth seeing, but at your own risk.

Sarge's Deli

548 Third Avenue (between 36th and 37th Streets)

212-679-0442

$ $

A sort of also-ran to New York's more famous delis, Sarge's has never managed to draw locals or tourists the way Second Avenue or Carnegie have. But that shouldn't discourage a solo diner from trying it, especially if you've got a craving for pastrami and pickles in the middle of the night (Sarge's is open twenty-four hours). It's also a good option on a weird, Twilight Zone stretch of Third Avenue. The Solo Diner has alway been warmly welcomed here, promptly seated, and chatted up by the motherly waitresses. There never seems to be a shortage of tables for one. The turkey sandwich he likes to order always comes heaped with more meat than he can ever hope to finish in one sitting. Soups are delicious, including an authentic-tasting matzoh ball. The room itself is brightly lit, familiar-looking, and just this side of charming (on the other side is shabby). Beer and wine are available, but who would order them here?

Sotto Cinque

417 Third Avenue (at 26th Street)

212-685-2037

$

Solo diners on a budget will appreciate that Sotto Cinque is best known in Murray Hill as "the place with the five-dollar pasta." The menu goes beyond that basic offering, with simple, well-prepared favorites like chicken marsala, veal scallopini, and calamari fra diavolo. The Solo Diner usually sticks to the more expensive pasta—in the $5 to $10 range—and does quite well with a tasty, filling, and inexpensive meal. Wine list is surprisingly extensive for a place like this, with selections from eleven Italian varietals (of middling quality, but that goes with the territory). Lighting good enough to read by. Claustrophobes, beware: the tables are small and you'll feel cramped even if the next nearest diner is three tables away. P.S. The uptown branch (see page 137) offers the same ludicrously low prices in a neighborhood where $5 sometimes won't buy a soda.

Tabla

11 Madison Avenue (at 25th Street)
212-889-0667

$ $ $ $

By rights, Tabla would be a gag restaurant, empty but for the sophisticated few who are in on the joke. In reality, Tabla is so crowded it is often difficult to get a table even at such traditional off hours as six or ten P.M. As with most Danny Meyer enterprises, great efforts are made to accommodate solo diners. The gag here is to take new American cuisine and prepare it with the spices and sensibility of the Indian subcontinent. The results are often as weird as they are wonderful. The Solo Diner found some crab cakes prepared with avocado, tamarind, and papadums a fascinating variation on a favorite theme. The downstairs Bread Bar, with a less expensive menu and more casual setting, offers another good option for a table for one. Fare includes such interesting items as rosemary naan with a tandoori lamb sauce, and a very upscale version of the traditional Indian thali tasting plate. Creating a wine list to complement Indian spices is dicey at best, and Tabla has done about as good a job as one can.

Tibetan Kitchen
444 Third Avenue (at 31st Street)
212-679-6286
$ 🍴 🍴 🍴 🍴
👤 👤 👤 👤
🍷 🍷 🍷 🍷   🏮 🏮 🏮 🏮

It doesn't get more real than this. Tibetan Kitchen claims to be the first Tibetan restaurant in North America. It's operated by a corporation whose owners identify them-selves as the "Tibetan government in exile." It's a small hole-in-the-wall restaurant serving authentic and delicious Himalayan dishes. Momos, the most popular, are Tibetan dumplings filled with beef or vegetables; The Solo Diner has also enjoyed tsel gutse-ritu, a kind of lamb stew served with noodles, and the Himalayan khatsa, a lethally spicy dish of cold vegetables and bread. Finish up with a bhatsa makhu—handmade pasta lightly rolled in brown sugar, grated cheese, and roasted barley flour. The Solo Diner has never seen the restaurant fill up and suspects there's always a table for those dining alone. No wine list, of course, but Tibetan buttered tea balances the experience here better anyway. Lighting is good for reading. Caveat: English is very much a second language here.

Tikka
344 Lexington Avenue (between 39th and 40th Streets)
212-370-4054

"If you like Tiffin and Thali, please stop in to Tikka," their website politely requests. And you should—not as a favor to the owners, but to yourself. The eldest in this troika of unusual Indian eateries was recently renovated for a cleaner, brighter look; it now boasts more small tables, making it a perfect choice for solo diners looking for something bolder than the Curry Hill standbys. How about tandoori lobster tails? Or Parta Ni Macchi, a delicious traditional Parsi-style dish of fish steamed in banana leaves? You'll find them here, along with standout versions of favorites like chicken tikka (greaseless), lamb vindaloo (slightly tamed for Western palates), and superb vegetarian dishes. Service is impeccable; lighting is very good.

Union Square Café

21 East 16th Street (between Fifth Avenue and Union Square West)

212-243-4020

$ $ $ $

Union Square Café is one of the most popular restaurants in New York and turns up regularly on lists of the top tables in New York in terms of both food and service. And it's still single-friendly, although it's best to come early or late. For about fifteen years now the Union Square Café has been serving new American cuisine in a pleasant atmosphere with exemplary service. Some critics, in fact, maintain it's the high level of professional service making customers feel comfortable and welcome that makes the restaurant. The food—which is really as good as it ever was—no longer seems as radical a departure from the norm, since many other establishments followed Union Square Café's lead and then surpassed it. Alas, those restaurants have not followed the Union Square Café in service, let alone surpassed it. There are over a dozen wines by the glass.

Won Jo

23 West 32nd Street (between Fifth and Sixth Avenues)
212-695-5815

$ $ 🍴 🍴 🍴 🍴

Won Jo was just about the first Korean restaurant in New York and remains among the busiest and more authentic. Solo diners are welcome here, but the portions tend to be large enough for two. Fun, even for one, is a Korean barbecue that you grill right at your table. Open twenty-four hours a day.

Zen Palate

34 Union Square East (at 16th Street)
212-614-9291

$ 🍴 🍴 🍴 🍴

The Union Square outpost of these very cool neo-Chinese eateries is home to one of the city's grooviest solo-dining scenes; dreadlocks, shaved heads, and goofy hats usually share the crowded counter with more mundanely attired locals and tourists. The other Zen Palate locations look equally cool, with their sleek interiors, but offer more laid-back environments. All locations serve the intriguing menu at the bar, as well as at copious small tables; "Zen" special-ties include whimsically named dishes like "Shredded Melody" and "Tasty Harmony," some of which contain the most realistic fake meats you've ever tasted. Major draw-back: interminable waits, especially in warmer months when the terrace opens at Union Square.

Curry Hill

Stroll down (or up) Lexington Avenue into the Twenties. Notice anything different? How about the Bollywood movie posters, the scent of curry wafting through open storefront doors, and the gentlemen in turbans and ladies in saris? Welcome to Murray Hill's "Curry Hill," one of Manhat-tan's Little Indias (the other, more touristy version is on East 6th Street between First and Second Avenues). It's a walk-ing tour in its own right—and a bonanza for adventure-some solo diners. Many of the restaurants on these blocks serve their delicacies cafeteria-style, which means they're ideal for solo diners; you'll occasionally share the experience with entire extended Indian families out for a splurge, which can add to the fun if you're in the mood. Even at the places with table service, The Solo Diner never felt less than enthusiastically welcomed. Among the restaurants themselves, cuisine varies from familiar favorites to spe-cialized regional cooking to kosher vegetarian. Best of all, it's nearly impossible to spend more than $20 at most of these places, no matter how hard you try. Among The Solo Diner's favorites:

Curry in a Hurry
119 Lexington Avenue (at 28th Street)
212-683-0900
$

Traditional, familiar curries, tikkas, and vindaloos, well-prepared in an idiosyncratic mint-green space. Indian music videos and movies play nonstop. Lots of kids. Cafeteria-style service prevails, but table service is available in the upstairs dining room. No liquor.

Madras Mahal
104 Lexington Avenue (at 27th Street)
212-684-4010
$

Southern Indian kosher vegetarian menu, along with some traditional favorites. Brightly lit, which makes it especially good for solo diners. Known for its dosas (Indian crepes filled with potatoes, onions, and peas, along with fillings of your choice), but sometimes greasy. Table service.

Mavalli Palace
46 East 29th Street (between Madison and Park Avenue South)
212-679-5535
$

Off the beaten Curry Hill track literally and figuratively, this bistrolike vegan features bright, subdued decor and a bar. Spicy vegetable patties, vegetables with chickpeas and pomegranate juice, and dosa all get raves. Table service.

Muriya

129 East 27th Street (between Park and Lexington)
212-689-7925
$ $

An expansive dining room and earnest table service—along with exceptionally prepared traditional favorites—help Muriya stand out. Samosas, tikkas, chapattis, Biryani basmati rice dishes, and lassis are all delicious here. Well-lighted room too.

Saffron

81 Lexington Avenue (at 26th Street)
212-696-5130
$

Only in New York: another kosher vegetarian, this time in a more upscale setting. Specialties include attractive thalis (Indian tasting plates), dosas, and delicious breads and lassis (cool yogurt drinks). Table service.

Shaheen Restaurant

99 Lexington Avenue (at 27th Street)
212-683-2323
$

Solid, reliable Indian and Pakistani. Specializes in Biryani cuisine, tandoori chicken, Pakistani-style kebabs, and karahi chicken, fish, shrimp, and lamb. Cafeteria-style service.

42ND STREET TO 59TH STREET
Midtown North

WITH THE UNITED Nations on one side of the island and Hell's Kitchen on the other, why wouldn't the Theater District be smack just left of center in this prime strip of Manhattan real estate?

The expensive business lunch and dinner places are not solo diner friendly. They may condescend to serve you, but it will likely be at the bar only. Hell's Kitchen has developed quite a restaurant row along Ninth Avenue—much safer and tastier than you could imagine—but the places tend to be small holes-in-the-wall. Most have no problem seating singles, but as the area or the restaurant goes up, the service to singles goes down. Also check out "Little Brazil" on West 46th Street. There may be a capirinha and a samba in your future.

The restaurants catering to theatergoers are often a solo diner's best bet. Look for early-bird or pretheater specials—a sure sign that the restaurant is trying to build business during slow hours. Also, many of those restaurants are overbooked before the curtain. When the theaters are full, the restaurants are empty—an excellent opportunity for solo diners who like dinner at eight.

Amy's Bread
672 Ninth Avenue (between 46th and 47th Streets)
212-977-2670
See page 64.

Aquavit
13 West 54th Street (between Fifth and Sixth Avenues)
212-307-7311
$ $ $

The highly acclaimed, dimly lit restaurant downstairs is forbidding for solo diners. But the bright upstairs café serves a simplified, less expensive version of chef Marcus Samuelsson's simple yet spectacular fish preparations, refreshing desserts, and, of course, Aquavit's namesake liquor, a strong Swedish brew fermented from potatoes. The Solo Diner still grows misty-eyed over a simple poached halibut entrée he experienced here, the most perfectly prepared piece of fish he has ever encountered. Service is attentive without hovering. If you're on an expense account or just in the mood for a solo splurge, there's no better place to run up a tab.

Bouterin
420 East 59th Street (between First Avenue and Sutton Place)
212-758-0323
$ $ $

Like many restaurants with New York's better tables, Bouterin is not solo diner allergic. In that Gallic way, the staff hides its true feelings—whatever they may be—under considerable charm. And that's kind of what this restaurant excels in: charm. There's the charm of the terrace that's open on balmy nights. There's the charm of the French Provençal decor. There's the charm of the Provençale cuisine. There's the charm of its casual clutter. And then there's the charm of the white bean soup, a tarte à la Provençale, and the beef daube. Open for dinner only, so time your meal strategically.

Brasserie

100 East 53rd Street (between Park and Lexington)
212-751-4840
$ $ $

Walking into Brasserie is a shock. A demure little sign and revolving doors don't prepare you for the sensory overload inside, where a luminous, gently sloping staircase leads you down through a narrow entrance into the buzzing, riotous dining area. Translucent light green tables, white walls, and a bank of televisions above the bar complete the space-odyssey ambience. At first glance Brasserie would appear to be most unhospitable to solo diners; it's very much a scene, and scene restaurants generally act like they have better things to do than accommodate tables for one. But this place delivers a very pleasant surprise. Even at busy lunch and dinner hours, The Solo Diner's seen at least one other solo diner happily savoring the bistro-with-a-twist cuisine (foie gras, onion tart, lobster salad, cassoulet, pot-au-feu, rabbit). If a table for one isn't available—and at peak hours it can be challenging—the long glass bar counter, with its squarish high-design "bar stools," offers an appealing alternative. The food is a bit heavy, but delicious. Service is well-choreographed, with a few "who-gets-the-soup" bumps. Lighting is excellent, as is the selection of wines by the glass. P.S. Brasserie first opened here, in the basement of the landmark Seagram Building, in 1959. Closed by a fire in 1995, it reopened in January 2000 in its present incarnation. P.P.S. Brasserie is the pick of solo-dining celebrity Roger Black (see page 122)!

Café Centro

200 Park Avenue (in the MetLife Building, between 45th Street and Vanderbilt Avenue)
212-818-1222

$ $ $

A nice shiraz—The Solo Diner's favorite wine—is rarely available anywhere by the glass. So he knew he was off to a good start when he settled into a well-lighted table for one at the cavernous, clubby, very popular Café Centro and spied his beloved varietal served that way on the menu (there's also an unusually wide selection of beers). Along with hyperefficient service and very good food, this added up to a worthwhile indulgence in a neighborhood whose only other solo-dining options are the stalls or splurges across the street at Grand Central. The preponderance of commuters and office workers here means that peak hours get reversed; it's near-impossible to get a table for one at lunchtime, but the place quiets down considerably after evening rush hour. As early as 7:30 P.M. on a weekday evening, The Solo Diner has had no trouble getting seated promptly. Watch the chefs in the expansive glassed-in kitchen as they prepare your roasted salmon, marinated tuna with artichokes, or barbecued baby chicken. One dessert is worth dropping the diet for: pounded figs with a little brown sugar and a balsamic vinegar glaze with a port wine gelée. You won't know what hit you.

Café SFA
Saks Fifth Avenue
611 Fifth Avenue (at 50th Street)
212-940-4080

As with most department store restaurants, Café SFA is very single diner friendly. The Solo Diner is an architecture buff, and he liked the eye-level views of the spires of St. Patrick's Cathedral that some tables at this new American cuisine café afford. Other views of the architecture along Fifth Avenue aren't shabby either, and for people-watchers there is the passing scene presented by Saks Fifth Avenue shoppers. And the food, including tasty salads and sandwiches, is good too.

Carnegie Deli
854 Seventh Avenue (at 55th Street)
212-757-2245

Yes, it's overrun with tourists, but this New York institution didn't get where it is for nothing. The sandwiches are as colossal as you've heard; the waiters are gruffer than you'd believe; and the decor is deli by way of Disney. That said, solo diners will find it weirdly welcoming. Though the seating consists entirely of communal tables, they don't feel so uninviting, probably because there's no other option. Fanatic egalitarianism here also means nobody gets treated better than anyone else, so solo diners are nudged as much as groups and couples. Lighting's terrific, and the people-watching makes for compelling anthropology.

Caviar Russe

538 Madison Avenue (between 54th and 55th Streets)
212-980-5908

$ $ $ $

If you're looking for an over-the-top splurge, a surprising number of solo diners claim this clublike midtowner as a haven for solo dining. The Solo Diner found it adequate on that count; he suspects the romance of caviar, opulent blue-and-white rooms, and a pro-smoking policy makes up for any lost ground. The star of the show is, of course, the caviar; The Solo Diner doesn't know beluga from Sevruga, but swooned over each of the varieties he tasted. He avoided the rare eggs that cost close to $1,000 per serving, though. The noncaviar menu is good nouvelle Russian, including smoked salmon with blini and a hefty seafood platter. The five-course tasting menu is a steal, relatively speaking.

Chin Chin

216 East 49th Street (between Second and Third Avenues)
212-888-4555

All Chinese restaurants in New York are good bets for solo diners, but Chin Chin (the choice of celeb solo diner Liz Smith) merits a special mention for elevating the experience. Don't be fooled by its blah decor and ambience; the service and food here are far superior to most neighborhood chopstick joints, and solo diners are warmly welcomed, even pampered. Shrimp with Grand Marnier sauce, Szechuan lobster, and noodle dishes all rate raves; all this quality, of course, comes at a price, so prepare yourself for an inflated tab.

City Chow Cafe (at Equinox Fitness Club)
Fifth Avenue at 43rd Street
212-972-8000

Broadway at 50th Street
212-541-7000

Second Avenue at 54th Street
212-277-5400
See page 71.

Columbus Bakery
957 First Avenue (between 52nd and 53rd Streets)
212-421-0034

You wouldn't guess, but Columbus Bakery is owned by Ark Restaurants, a chain with diverse outposts in such far-flung locales as Florida and California. Normally, The Solo Diner would flee for that reason alone. But the folks at Ark seem to have found a winning formula at these three bakeries-cum-hangouts (see pages 9 and 144 for other locations). This First Avenue location and the one on the Upper West Side are bright and relaxed, with round marble-topped tables amply spaced from each other. Along with generously proportioned mugs of great coffee, you'll find pastries, desserts, and full menus for breakfast through to dinner. Sandwiches, like roast beef and grilled veggies, are tasty but soggy; The Solo Diner suspects they came from a central kitchen. Salads like a nutty multigrain and a tangy Israeli couscous are fresh, if a little heavy, while pizzas are hot and light and crepes perfectly prepared. Best of all, these places unconsciously encourage lingering; they're spread-out-the-newspaper kinds of environments, which solo diners don't see enough of in New York. P.S. An innovation other places could learn from: there's a tiny wine rack near the entrance whose six well-chosen occupants comprise the by-the-glass wine list.

Comfort Diner

214 East 45th Street (between Second and Third Avenues)

212-867-4555

$ 🍴 🍴 🍴

Along with its younger sibling (see page 129), this retro mid-towner serves up faithful renditions of classic diner favorites like meat loaf, macaroni and cheese, fried chicken, and milk shakes. They also revive the classic diner tradition of respecting solo customers. Though service can be a little lackadaisical, especially at the midtown branch, the waiters and waitresses here work hard to make you feel, well, comfortable, and try their best to act like everyone's a regular. The 45th Street location is an oasis in a part of midtown where those frightening deli salad bars seem to vastly outnumber decent restaurants. Breakfast is especially enjoyable at both outposts, though weekend brunch can get packed. Watch for silly but fun promotions like the recent "Month of Milk Shakes," which featured s'mores, creamsicle, blueberry cheesecake, black licorice, and other alarming flavors. P.S. Upper East Side branch has full bar with very small selection of wines by the glass.

Cosi/Xando
61 West 48th Street (between Fifth and Sixth Avenues)
212-265-2674

Paramount Plaza
1633 Broadway (between 51st and 52nd Streets)
212-397-2674

38 East 45th Street (between Madison and Vanderbilt)
212-949-7400

165 East 52nd Street (near Third Avenue)
212-758-7800

60 East 56th Street (between Madison and Park)
212-588-0888

11 West 42nd Street (between Fifth and Sixth Avenues)
212-398-6660
See page 9.

Cupcake Café

522 Ninth Avenue (between 38th and 39th Streets)

212-465-1530

$ 〃 〃 〃 〃 〃

👤 👤 👤

💡 💡 💡 💡 💡 🪑 🪑 🪑 🪑 🪑

The Solo Diner lived on 37th Street at Ninth Avenue when he got out of college. This was before New Times Square; in fact, it was extremely Old Times Square. Taxi drivers would refuse to drop him in front of his building, fearing for their lives. How things have changed. Ninth Avenue in the Thirties has undergone a renaissance of sorts, and Cupcake Café helped start it. There's nothing fancy about the place; you'll see a dinerlike exterior, simple display cases, and some mismatched tables that tend to get jumbled by the end of the day. The homemade soups and sandwiches are hearty and delicious, the muffins and donuts are irresistible, and the coffee's strong. Lighting is ideal for reading, and there are a couple of tables for one along with two four-tops. Counter help can be brusque. Grab a table by the front window and watch Ninth Avenue pass by in all its weird glory. P.S. Cupcake Café is revered around the world for its mind-blowing cakes—they're more like rococo architecture than baking. You'll see patrons pulling up in cabs and limos to pick them up all day long.

Firebird

365 West 46th Street (between Eighth and Ninth Avenues)

212-586-0244

$ $ $ 〃 〃 〃

👤 👤 👤 👤 👤 🍸 🍸 🍸

💡 💡 🪑 🪑

Firebird is where people who loved the Russian Tea Room went (after the old Russian Tea Room was coopted by the tourist trade). It's champagne, it's caviar—not to mention borscht and blini—it's waiters dressed as Cossacks, and other Czarist indulgences. It's so over the top, it transcends camp and becomes scrumptious. The vodka list, needless to say, is more impressive than the wine list. Solo dining here isn't as much fun as it is in a group, but timed right, it's still an experience, and the service is solicitous.

Joe's Shanghai

24 West 56th Street (between Fifth and Sixth Avenues)
212-333-3868
See page 11.

Judson Grill

152 West 52nd Street (between Sixth and Seventh Avenues)
212-582-5252

$ $ $ 🍴 🍴 🍴 🍴

🍸 🍸 🍸 🍸 🍷 🍷 🍷

🪑 🪑 🪑 🪑 🪑 🪑

Judson Grill (that's an old New York phone exchange, not a typo) is primarily a business lunch and after-work place, which can make it a bit daunting for timid single diners. However, this well-established new American cuisine restaurant is very solo-friendly, which helps make the gargantuan room a little less intimidating. Dishes are seasonal: Peeky-toe crab cocktail with caviar and avocado; Maine halibut, and a Jack Daniel's chocolate ice cream soda are perennial favorites here. (There's also a chocolate sampler for the non-drinking chocoholic.)

La Bonne Soupe

48 West 55th Street (between Fifth and Sixth Avenues)

212-586-7650

$ $

The Solo Diner has fond memories of solo lunches here at breaks from his first real job. French lite, rather than light French, cuisine; lunches of soups and salads are supplemented by such heartier fare as cassoulet and coq au vin. A bit genteel shabby now, but for devotees, it's forever chic. The atmosphere is pleasant and the service prompt enough. Women and solo diners will all feel welcome here.

Local

224 West 47th Street (between Broadway and Eighth Avenue)

212-921-1005

$ $ $ $

Before you reserve a table for one at this sleek young midtowner, consider the long, well-lighted chef's counter instead. The comfy stools give solo diners an ideal perch to watch the busy open kitchen, and chef Franklin Becker may even offer a quick discourse on whatever you've ordered. There's a lot for him to talk about; Becker is very serious about his "evolved New York cuisine," and simple names on the menu belie complex preparations with precise ingredients (though some, like "grilled day boat halibut," may offer too much information). They come together beautifully in dishes like ginger-scented borscht, tuna tartare, hamachi sashimi, and pan-seared wolffish. Desserts are jaw-dropping, especially the banana toffee cake with sour cream–banana ice cream. Diverse selection of wines by the glass. A gripe: stratospheric prices sometimes accompany smallish portions. "It's a local place, evolved, for the new laborer in New York," according to the menu. Yeah, right, if the "laborer" toils on Wall Street. That said, it's hard to do better for a Theater-District splurge.

Margon Restaurant

136 West 46th Street (between Sixth and Seventh Avenues)

212-354-5013

$

It resembles nothing more than a deli on the outside, with its yellow and blue sign and neon Budweiser logo in the window. Actually, from the inside it's nothing special either, just standard Formica and vinyl. But this minuscule lunch counter has developed quite a reputation among the cognoscenti as having some of the city's best Cuban food. Copious portions—The Solo Diner dares you to finish one—of rice and beans accompany home-cooked octopus salad, pot roast, and Cuban sandwiches. The fried plantains are to die for, and the espresso is rich and strong. Unlike Cuba itself, service can be democratic, to put it politely; this might not be the place for anyone seeking special treatment. The Solo Diner even makes an exception to his communal table rule (avoid them) for this place, where sharing a table is mandatory. Lighting is bright, but there's not much room to read. No wine list, but as the sign in the window promises, there's beer.

Mitchel London Foods

542 Ninth Avenue (between 39th and 40th Streets)

212-563-5969

$ $

The Solo Diner was surprised when Mitchel London Foods, which operates a fancy-shmancy catering and takeout joint on Madison Avenue, opened a small, spare, but airy café/shop at the very downmarket corner of 40th and Ninth back in 1998. Mr. London must have known something The Solo Diner doesn't, because this charming spot is thriving. Since Mitchel London Foods is next to the Port Authority Bus Terminal, it may be that people are making special trips for the food here; you won't doubt it once you taste the soulful chicken soup, or a perfectly roasted half chicken, or a heavenly moist yellow cupcake. Solo diners will appreciate the friendly counter service, small tables, and good lighting. Unparalleled people-watching, of the Diane Arbus variety, on Ninth Avenue. Get here before the tourists discover it.

Morrell Wine Bar & Café

16 West 49th Street (1 Rockefeller Plaza, between Fifth and Sixth Avenues)

212-262-7700

$ $ $

Solo oenophiles, rejoice: the wine list at Morrell Wine Bar & Café includes more than 120 selections available by the glass. It's the offspring of Morrell & Company, the famous family-owned wine and spirits company that recently relocated here after more than fifty years uptown. And it was worth waiting that long for its pricey but welcoming offspring, just next door. A soaring, bilevel space, Morrell is unusual for this neighborhood not only for its stylishness (the space is all sensuous curves), but for the warm welcome it extends solo diners. It may be tough to snare a table during peak hours. But the wine bar, where a full menu is served, offers a perfect perch to take in the scene—all business at lunch, more intimate at dinner. Lighting at the bar is good, adequate elsewhere. Asian-inflected menu is simple but luxurious, like watercress salad with figs, Gorgonzola and poached Chilean sea bass, and stir-fried lobster.

Oceana
55 East 54th Street (between Madison and Park)
212-759-5941
$ $ $ $

The decor echoes an ocean liner (without degenerating into being a theme park), which is a bit of a metaphor for the use of Asian, Mediterranean, and other ethnic seasonings applied to fresh seafood. The menu changes daily, but typical offerings include lobster ravioli in a basil tomato broth, crab cakes with chipotle chili sauce, and seared blackfish. Service is smooth, and there is a range of prix fixe options. And if you have forgotten to bring something to read, there's always the forty-five-page wine list.

Ollie's Midtown
190 West 44th Street (between Broadway and Eighth Avenue)
212-921-5988

Not that it was ever a gourmand's paradise, but the Theater District is a victim of its own popularity. There are very few places west of Ninth Avenue where a solo diner would feel comfortable, or even welcome. Ollie's isn't exactly a remedy, but it's fast, cheap, and casual enough to make solo diners feel like they belong; despite the subway-at-rush-hour atmosphere, The Solo Diner's never had a problem getting a table. There are basically two food groups here, dumplings and noodles. Both come alone or in soups, and you can't go wrong with them. The Solo Diner's partial to the clear broth with chicken, scallions, and slurpy noodles, as well as the steamed green dumplings. Sample more exotic fare at your own risk. Service is hyperefficient and unsmiling, but not unfriendly; wines are of the screw-top variety. P.S. Avoid pretheater times if you value your sanity.

Oyster Bar
Grand Central Station
212-490-6650

$ $ $

♀ ♀ ♀ ♀

🍴 🍴 🍴 🍴

Ⅰ Ⅰ Ⅰ Ⅰ Ⅰ

🪑 🪑 🪑

The problem with the Oyster Bar is not how it treats solo diners—which is quite well, especially at its oyster bar. And it's not the wine list, which obviously puts the emphasis on white and offers some eighty different wines by the glass. It's not even the food, which includes many impeccable fish preparations. The problem with the Oyster Bar is the glockenspiel effect created by a crowded restaurant whose walls are tiled parabolic arches. It makes concentrating on a magazine difficult; The Solo Diner can't imagine conversing here. The crowd is mixed, part business, part tourist. Avoid dining too late, when the restaurant seems filled with older businessmen trying to impress young prey—unless you enjoy observing that kind of thing.

Petrossian

182 West 58th Street (at Seventh Avenue)

212-245-2214

$ $ $ $

The Solo Diner is amazed at the number of caviar joints solo-dining friends recommended. Petrossian is another in the Czarist fantasy school of caviar emporia, although here the Czar made it to art deco. Many feel Petrossian is the best of the lot. It is certainly among the most affordable. Caviar here is served on warm toast, blini, and small spoons. Vodka is in iced flutes. Although there's more to Petrossian than caviar—the cuisine offered is, after all, Franco-Russian—you're left feeling the place is less about food than atmosphere, more about being seen than being served. Petrossian emphasizes the conspicuous in the conspicuous consumption of food.

Sandwich Planet

534 Ninth Avenue (between 39th and 40th Streets)

212-273-9768

$

Like other young eateries in this area, Sandwich Planet is minuscule, charming, and earnest in its desire to please. The gimmick here is the ready-made sandwich elevated to an art form. The menu features more than a hundred of them, with ingredients ranging from pedestrian favorites like ham, cheese, and lettuce to Toscano salami, fontina, horseradish, jalapenos, and oven-roasted beef. Everything's overstuffed and served on luscious breads; classics like grilled cheese are transformed into something transcendent. The place itself is minuscule, with only three tables, all two-tops perfect for solo diners. Avoid the lunch rush and a seat shouldn't be a problem. Beer is available.

Sushisay

38 East 51st Street (between Fifth and Sixth Avenues)
212-755-1780
$ $ $

Sushisay's deep dark secret is that it's actually a chain whose other outlets are all back in Tokyo, where the chefs are trained. However, it's the quality of the place that draws both a Japanese and American crowd. The best fish is at the bar itself (the best of the best go to those who know how to use chopsticks). Ultimately, however, it's a lunch place for businesspeople on expense accounts. All sushi bars are single dining friendly, but this one deserves special mention for efficiency that matches the excellence of the fish.

Sushiya

28 West 56th Street (between Fifth and Sixth Avenues)
212-247-5760

$ $

Sushiya is a sushi bar that disproves the engineer's rule of thumb that something can't be fast, good, and cheap. Decor and service can be best described as minimalist.

Trattoria Dell'Arte
900 Seventh Avenue (at 57th Street)
212-245-9800
$ $ $

On a theater night—in other words, any night but Sunday and Monday—don't even think of venturing in here between the hours of six and eight P.M., when the preshow crowds mob this place. It's one of the few reliable, worth-the-price establishments in this tourist-heavy area. But if you find yourself in the neighborhood during off-peak hours, you'll be charmed by the attentive service, whimsical decor (themed around noses, for some inexplicable reason), and terrific cuisine here. The Solo Diner has enjoyed wonderful meals at the bar, with solicitous, talky bartenders doubling as efficient and informed waiters; he actually prefers it to tables, though the dining-room lighting is perfect. The food is great, though the kitchen occasionally stumbles on busy nights. A solo diner could make a satisfying meal of the antipasto plate here—The Solo Diner has—but then you'd miss out on the elegant thin-crust pizzas, chicken paillard, and impeccably cooked fish specials. A generous selection of wines by the glass is also available.

Wollensky's Grill

205 East 49th Street (at Third Avenue)

212-753-0444

$ $ $

Its legendary namesake next door, Smith & Wollensky, is a bit too much for The Solo Diner's taste. Steaks, murky decor, boys' club ambience, and enormous tabs there all feel very heavy. But this lighter, friendlier sibling makes an appealing stop for carnivores. If you can tolerate unwavering noise and a packed room, you'll find excellent service and a full menu at the bar, including the duly famous creamed spinach, hash brown potatoes, juicy burgers—and those Flintstones-like steaks—at more easily digested prices.

Zen Palate

663 Ninth Avenue (at 46th Street)

212-582-1669

See page 90.

Hotel Restaurants

Hotel restaurants have always been havens for solo diners. A preponderance of business travelers has always meant at least a couple of solo diners in any hotel restaurant.

But hotel dining used to mean generic, overpriced food in glorified coffee shops.

Not anymore. Today, you'll find some of New York's most intriguing restaurants inside its lodging properties. It was once unthinkable, but locals are partaking shoulder-to-shoulder with the tourists.

On the one hand, that's good news if you're seeking a table for one. The excitement in hotel kitchens means standards keep rising. The downside is that the hotter they get, many hotel dining rooms become less hospitable to solo diners (at the bustling lobby restaurant in the self-consciously hip Tribeca Grand, The Solo Diner was treated as if he literally did not exist). Here are a few choices where The Solo Diner was mostly received as a welcome guest rather than an unwanted pest:

An American Place

The Benjamin Hotel
125 East 50th Street (at Lexington Avenue)
212-888-5650

$ $ $ $

While this contemporary restaurant—owned by legendary chef Larry Forgione—doesn't officially belong to the Benjamin, it makes a nice complement to the hotel's casual chic. There are too many big tables to make it very welcoming for solo diners, but the finely tuned service (especially at dinner, when the place quiets down) and wonderful food make up for it. Forgione's calling card is simple but exuberant regional American cuisine, and his cedar-plank salmon, grilled free-range chicken breast, and "tuna mignon" make you share his enthusiasm. Fine selection of wines by the glass; lighting is adequate.

Avalon Bar & Grill

The Avalon Hotel
16 East 32nd Street (between Madison and Fifth)
212-299-7000

$ $ $

This intimate, slightly dark restaurant inside a newish hotel in the shadow of the Empire State Building offers a menu based on organic ingredients—apparently from a very expensive farm. Very solicitous, if slightly confused, service. Simple but impeccable preparations include an heirloom tomato salad and grilled octopus starters, and main dishes of Thai snapper, yellowfin tuna, and duck breast. It remains undiscovered among locals, so you very well may get a large table to yourself at peak hours.

Café Botanica

Essex House
160 Central Park South (between Sixth and Seventh Avenues)
212-484-5120

$ $ $

If you're looking for a hotel dining room with a view, this is it; you'll find lovely views of Central Park. It's tranquil; it's elegant; it's French Provençal. The clean, modern menu and smooth service save it from stuffiness. The Solo Diner was even seated at a table for four at the tail end of lunchtime one weekday. He enjoyed, as an appetizer, a refined lobster salad in pomegranate vinaigrette, then a delicate poached halibut entrée, and finished with a warm peach tart that inspired thoughts of summer somewhere in the country. The waitstaff here, attentive without hovering, is clearly accustomed to serving solo diners.

Canal House

Soho Grand
310 West Broadway (at Grand Street)
212-965-3000

$ $ $

Unbearable when it first opened, a victim of its own hype, this place has finally settled into a comfortable groove of smooth service, excellent food, and relaxed ambience. The Solo Diner's main complaint here remains the lighting, a holdover from Canal House's days as a scene. But the subtle, pretty room has plenty of tables suitable for one, and the "regional cuisine with a Yankee flair" makes it worth a visit. The macaroni and cheese (made with aged cheddar) deserves its lofty reputation, and the horseradish-crusted halibut is invigorating. Only five (count 'em) wines by the glass, but all are very fine.

Carlyle Restaurant

Carlyle Hotel
35 East 76th Street (at Madison Avenue)
212-744-1800
$ $ $

Now that the Rainbow Room is closed, this is where The Solo Diner goes to fulfill fantasies inspired by Fred Astaire/Ginger Rogers movies of New York sophistication. Timed right, you can shamelessly indulge all your cinematic fantasies of New York. Marble walls, huge floral displays, and lush banquettes set the tone for a menu that presents one perfectly prepared French-accented dish after another. Superb service is old-fashioned in the best possible sense; selection of wine by the glass is impeccable. The vibe is businesslike at lunch, romantic at dinner, but not so much of either that The Solo Diner felt put off. This is one place where the experience justifies the tab, especially for a solo diner.

C3 Restaurant

Washington Square Hotel
103 Waverly Place (at MacDougal Street)
212-979-8373
$ $ $

More locals than tourists seem to frequent this basement restaurant found in a charming West Village hotel. They come here for the impeccable food rather than the decor, which is warm and casual (black, wood, beige) but slightly generic. The menu, however, is distinguished, with simple ingredients flawlessly prepared. An endive salad with Stilton, bacon, walnuts, and onions is irresistible; Asian spring rolls with mango and jicama are a lively surprise; and a pan-seared tuna with quinoa is perfectly cooked and beautifully presented. You'll find a nice setup for solo diners, with quite a few small tables; the place rarely gets packed, which means you can kick back, relax, focus on your reading, and hear yourself think. Small wine list; good lighting. P.S. Brunch here is phenomenal and doesn't draw the marauding hordes that raid other neighborhood places.

Fifty Seven Fifty Seven

The Four Seasons Hotel New York
57 East 57th Street (between Madison and Park Avenues)
212-758-5757
$ $ $ $

If you're a solo diner on an unlimited expense account, this is your place. While it aims for some kind of restrained opulence, everything about The Four Seasons is so nineties-New York-over-the-top (including its clientele) that you'll barely be able to focus on your reading material. Survey the I. M. Pei–designed lobby dining room as you feast on impeccably prepared yellowfin tuna carpaccio, conch chowder, or sushi/sashimi combination appetizers, and jerked chicken, grilled shrimp with basmati rice, or market-fresh fish entrées. The warm peach tart is a revelation. Annoyingly small but well-chosen selection of wines by the glass; good lighting throughout the day.

44

Royalton Hotel
44 West 44th Street
212-944-4484

$ $ $

"44" is invoked in these pages only because it represents the antithesis of what a hotel dining room should be. That is, where it should be welcoming to singles and travelers, it tests their patience and self-esteem. The Solo Diner should have known better. Despite 44's attitude-central reputation, he decided to treat himself to birthday dinner there—solo, of course. The gloomy, belligerent, lost-looking staff did everything they could to ruin his solitary festivities. Seated at a most unpleasant table in the middle of the room, he was left to his own devices; like a seldom-seen comet, a server or busboy would cruise by to drop a plate or sneer at a request for water. The food, not surprisingly, matched the service and tatty Philippe Starck decor. Soup was tepid, fish overcooked, vegetables lifeless. And none of this came cheap. You've been warned; even if you're staying there, find alternatives.

La Caravelle

Shoreham Hotel
33 West 55th Street (between Fifth and Sixth Avenues)
212-586-4252

$ $ $ $

The Solo Diner is occasionally hard-put to explain a passion for prix fixe. Aside, that is, from a prix fixe option being one index as to whether a place is suitable for solo dining. For the record, La Caravelle, a real old-guard classic French restaurant, offers at least four: lunch, dinner, tastings, and pretheater. Solo diners are treated with utmost care at all of them. Although it's in a hotel, La Caravelle is not exactly the hotel dining room. The room is pretty and the lighting might be best described as flattering. The service is handled by skilled professionals—something of a relief in New York, where food service is too often a euphemism for out-of-work performer. Any French classic is good here, but fish seems to be a specialty. Try sole meunière, crab cakes with corn, or even duck à l'orange. Offerings are seasonal.

Mark's

The Mark Hotel
25 East 77th Street (between Fifth and Madison)
212-879-1864

$ $ $ ⑂ ⑂ ⑂ ⑂

🛐 🛐 🛐 🛐   ⑂ ⑂

👥 👥 👥   👥 👥 👥 👥

The room looks dark and discreet—something somewhere
between a gentleman's club and deco cocktail lounge. Well,

Celebrity Sound Bite

I've always found the best tables for one in New York
are in the hotels—where single diners (particularly
women) do not stand out as much, and you can get
away with reading your book more easily.

Historically, the best was the Sherry Café (which
sadly was replaced by Cipriani, then some other
Eurotrash hangout). The Carlyle takes its place. Four
Seasons has a grand room, if chilly. The Waldorf has
a number of choices. But avoid the Hilton and the
other chains.

Outside of the hotels, the only places I like are
the Oyster Bar in Grand Central (page 110) and the
new Brasserie (page 97).

—Roger Black
Media design guru; chairman,
Danilo Black, Inc.

hotel dining should be discreet. And the room isn't all that dark. There's enough light to read by. The effect is proper and dignified. The food and service is also proper and dignified. Crab cakes, medallions of veal, and black and white chocolate gateaux St. Honoré—as well as other Franco-American offerings with Asian/Mediterranean touches. There are prix fixe menus for the brunch and pretheater crowd.

Peacock Alley

Waldorf-Astoria Hotel
301 Park Avenue (at 50th Street)
212-872-4895

$ $ $ $

Once staid and sleepy, now the gold standard for hotel dining, this fabled room has been rejuvenated by chef Laurent Gras. For solo diners looking to splurge, there's no better place to spend your money, inside or outside a hotel. The clockwork-precise service, hushed but relaxed atmosphere, and revelatory cooking make it worth every penny. Even better, the lighting's terrific, there are plenty of smaller tables, and the staff acts as if you're a respected regular at your usual table. The menu—divided by "category" rather than portion, jettisoning "appetizers" and "entrées" per se—changes frequently. Recent triumphs include heady lobster soup flavored with chestnuts, sea bass with black truffles, Dover sole with polenta, and rack of lamb—all simple but perfect. Desserts are mandatory, especially the quartet of apple desserts, if it's available. The abridged, overpriced list of wines by the glass is about the only drawback here.

60TH STREET TO 96TH STREET
The Upper East Side

MUSEUM MILE is here. So are Barneys, Bergdorf, and Bloomingdale's, not to mention the antique shops and designer boutiques along Madison and Lexington Avenues. The Upper East Side also has some of New York's best hotels. Yet solo dining can be a daunting experience. The heirs to Mortimer's—Swifty's (1007 Lexington Avenue), one where Mortimer's was, and even a new restaurant with the old name—are solo diner friendly only if the solo diner in question went to the right schools. (They all claim to have less exclusionary seating policies.)

The best choices are the excellent restaurants in such department stores as Barneys and Bloomingdale's—many people who shop alone take their shopping break alone—followed by the restaurants or snack shops in the Metropolitan Museum or the Whitney. It may not always be table service, but the food is better than average and no one minds if you linger. The hotels are of course always a best bet for solo dining.

On the other hand, many of the bars and restaurants that line Third and Second Avenues, while solo-tolerant, are glorified, if discreet, singles scenes. However, while the game is afoot, those places remain more welcoming of solo diners than some of the small exquisite and expensive boites that line many of the side streets.

Abajour

1134 First Avenue (between 62nd and 63rd Streets)

212-644-9757

$ $ $

This frozen-in-amber stretch of First Avenue dominated by the 59th Street Bridge is finally coming alive; a stylish home furnishings emporium, gigantic restaurant, and chic mega-supermarket all opened within months of each other in 1999. Now, Abajour has raised the bar for style in this neighborhood again with a relaxed, cream-colored dining room, late-night hours, and service that's more downtown informal than uptown stuffy. Though a scene evolves here every evening, it's not obnoxious, and the room's intimate, romantic vibe is understated enough that it shouldn't put off solo diners. There are several small tables where singles are accommodated warmly; settle in and enjoy the seafood-heavy appetizers (steamed mussels, oysters, and a mixed "shellfish plateau") and more diverse entrées (delicious roasted salmon fillet, rack of lamb, mixed seafood ravioli). Smaller selection of wines by the glass than you'd expect from such a bistrolike establishment. Lighting is fine (abajour means "lamp shade" in French, after all).

Annie's

1381 Third Avenue (between 78th and 79th Streets)

212-327-4853

$ $

The usual warning applies to this laid-back hangout, brought to you by restaurant mini-magnate Jim McMullen: avoid the weekend brunch apocalypse (noise, lines, strollers, cell phones) by any means necessary. The rest of the week, you can enjoy a relatively inexpensive breakfast, lunch, or dinner at one of the many small tables here with little fuss or fanfare. The Solo Diner prefers sitting against the wall on the right as you walk in; lighting is better in the front than in the back. Servers are young and energetic and seem to have mastered the difficult art of knowing when to leave solo diners alone as well as when to cater to them. The menu's straightforward: sandwiches (from a tuna melt and BLT to marinated leg of lamb with chutney), salads, burgers, pastas, and entrées like chicken breast with garlic, grilled salmon, and surprisingly good steak. Waffles and French toast at breakfast are textbook-perfect.

California Pizza Kitchen

201 East 60th Street (at Third Avenue)

212-755-7773

$

This is an East Coast branch of the famous West Coast chain of casual restaurants serving "designer" pizza. Essentially, it's a New-Age approach in which your pizza is topped with any-thing and everything except what you might find in your lo-cal traditional pizzeria: Thai chicken, Hawaiian pineapple, and who knows what other concoctions. Detractors feel the California Pizza Kitchen belongs in a mall in the sticks, not in New York's Upper East Side. The Solo Diner points out that solo diners are welcome here and the food is decent. So get over it and get in touch with your inner mall rat.

Candle Café

1307 Third Avenue (between 74th and 75th Streets)
212-472-0970

$ $ 🍴 🍴 🍴 🍴 🍴

🗽 🗽 🗽 🗽 🗽   🍸 🍸

🛎 🛎 🛎 🛎 🛎   🪑 🪑 🪑 🪑

You might wonder what spaceship dropped this place in the middle of the Upper East Side. It's cool, airy, comfortable, casual, and vegetarian, all anomalous qualities in this part of town. Even more rare, the young waitstaff is friendly, funny, and sweet to solo and nonsolo diners alike. The cui-sine is so good, even nonvegetarians will enjoy it, includ-ing the Crystal Roll appetizer (grilled tofu, vegetables, and rice noodles wrapped in rice paper), quesadilla, vegan lasagna, and a very tasty traditional Indian plate. The banana "cream" pie is a must-have, and the juices (mixed greens, apple, lemon, and ginger is a favorite) are killer.

City Chow Cafe (at Equinox Fitness Club)

Third Avenue at 86th Street
212-439-8500

Lexington Avenue at 63rd Street
212-750-4900
See page 71.

Celebrity Sound Bite

My favorite place to go to alone is Elaine's (page 130)—because Elaine Kaufman always sets aside what she calls "the family table," for regulars who come in on their own or haven't made a reservation.

—Cyndi Stivers
president and editor in chief,
Time Out New York magazine

Comfort Diner
142 East 86th Street (at Lexington Avenue)
212-369-8628
See page 102.

EJ's Luncheonette
1271 Third Avenue (at 73rd Street)
212-472-0600
See page 38.

El Pollo
1746 First Avenue (between 90th and 91st Streets)
212-996-7810
$

It's not much of a restaurant—more like a takeout counter with seats—but that's precisely why this tiny Peruvian barbecue spot is so perfect for solo diners. Add their perfectly marinated and roasted chicken and just-right fries and you've got a cheap, very memorable solo-dining experience. The place is always well-lighted, and the counter help is friendly. P.S. A new SoHo location (482 Broome Street; 212-431-5666) is larger and slicker, but lacks the authenticity and warmth of the original.

Elaine's

1703 Second Avenue (between 88th and 89th Streets)
212-534-8103

$ $ $

The first thing to understand about Elaine's is that no one comes here for the so-so Italian food. It's all about the scene, and dining solo here can give you a good perch from which to appreciate it. The Solo Diner has never figured out exactly why or how, but Elaine's is packed with celebrities on any given night, from Woody Allen to Ed Koch to John Lydon (enjoying cocktails one night, to The Solo Diner's shock). Elaine Kaufman, who owns the place, is supposedly a terror on two legs if she doesn't think you're important, but The Solo Diner has never encountered her fearsome presence; in fact, the waiters he's dealt with have always been courteous and friendly. There's a comfortable bar where the service is warm even if they don't recognize you. Solo diners may have a tougher time with tables at peak hours, though The Solo Diner has managed to score one on a few occasions. The side room off the main entrance is apparently known as Siberia, so kick and scream if they seat you there. Oh, the food . . . basics like chicken and pasta are safe, though the kitchen did turn out some very respectable lamb chops on a recent visit. Unimpressive wine list. This is where celebrity solo diner Cyndi Stivers, editor in chief of *Time Out New York* magazine, kicks back!

Fred's at Barneys NY

10 East 61st Street (near Madison Avenue)

212-833-2200

$ $

The lighting is good enough to read by, but this is really a place to watch the chic meet to eat. Catering to Barneys shoppers—solo or in packs—Fred's offers what might best be described as nouvelle American-Jewish Italian. Choices include a latke with lox and caviar, warm lobster salad, and linzer torte. You'll see many solo diners here, some laden with signature black Barneys shopping bags. Service presumes you're a solo diner of leisure.

Heidelberg

1648 Second Avenue (between 85th and 86th Streets)

212-682-2332

$ $

This is one of the last of the authentic, old-style German restaurants in Yorkville. It's wurst, Wiener schnitzel, and strudel as well as more German beer than you can possibly imagine. It's also quite noisy, but then again, shouldn't a beer garden be just that? Very welcoming of solo diners.

Ideal Restaurant

238 East 86th Street (between Second and Third Avenues)

212-535-0950

$ $ 🍴 🍴 🍴 🍴

👤 👤 👤 👤   🍸 🍸 🍸

👤 👤 👤 👤 👤   🪑 🪑 🪑 🪑

Like its neighbor, Heidelberg, Ideal is an endangered species. Here's hoping it soldiers on for many years. Back in college, The Solo Diner worked weekends at a nearby bookstore. Thoughts of a cheap meal here kept him going throughout the day. After work, he'd settle into one of the many small tables with a newspaper and let one of the matronly waitresses take care of him. The servers are no longer so matronly, the prices have climbed, and the place has been renovated. But the warm welcome's unchanged, as is the food—dense, delicious renditions of traditional Teutonic fare like Wiener schnitzel, goulash, and grilled meat platter, along with mandatory sides like German potato salad, dumplings, red cabbage, and spaetzle. Desserts include a torpedo-like apple strudel. Lighting's terrific, and there's a good selection of beer and a couple of German wines by the glass.

Jackson Hole Burgers

1270 Madison Avenue (at 91st Street)

212-427-2820

1611 Second Avenue (between 83rd and 84th Streets)

212-737-7187

232 East 64th Street (between Second and Third Avenues)
212-371-7187
$ 🍴 🍴 🍴 🍴

👤 👤 👤 👤

🪑 🪑 🪑 🪑 🪑   🏠 🏠 🏠 🏠 🏠

The first of these burger shrines—and havens for solo diners—first appeared on the Upper East Side nearly thirty years ago. Jackson Hole has since multiplied, but its formula remains singular: massive hunks of impeccably fresh ground beef (or turkey) served on soft, warm buns, with perfect fries and crunchy pickles. What else do you need? There's zero atmosphere at all of the locations, which is fine; no one comes to Jackson Hole for the ambience. But if you're in a carnivorous mood, want to taste a New York tradition, and want to be served by waitresses with a finely developed sense of when to leave solo diners alone, you'll want to try these places.

Le Train Bleu
Bloomingdale's
1000 Third Avenue (at 58th Street)
212-705-2100
$ $ 🍴 🍴 🍴

👤 👤   🍸 🍸

🪑 🪑 🪑   🏠 🏠 🏠 🏠

As with most department store restaurants, solo diners, whatever language they pretend to speak, are welcome here. The Solo Diner was sitting at one of Le Train Bleu's small tables when a handsome waiter came up and asked in a thick, almost unintelligible French accent what he wanted to order. Knowing that there are as many accents and dialects in French as there are in English, The Solo Diner decided it would be simpler to order in French than to repeat an order two or three times in English. The waiter was an out-of-work actor practicing his accents. OK, so this is a place less for francophone than francophonies, but the theme—a dining car on an old-fashioned luxury train—is a good use of a long narrow space. And it's a nice touch of nostalgia for those of us who are old enough to remember when dining cars on trains had linen tablecloths, flatware with heft, and real food. The vaguely French food here ranges from good to good enough.

Matthew's
1030 Third Avenue
212-838-4343
$ $ $

The open, circular layout of this sleek East Midtowner suits The Solo Diner's taste perfectly—as do the warm welcome, solicitous service, and perfectly balanced attention from waitstaff. Banquettes curve around the walls of the mauve-and-pink dining room, ensuring a sense of private space without isolating tables. Slightly dim lighting makes reading a chore at dinner, so scope out the strategically placed tables near light fixtures. Star chef Matthew Kenney's fascinating Mideast-influenced menu can be startling, from spiced pumpkin soup to tuna tartare with green-olive tapenade.

Payard Patisserie & Bistro
1032 Lexington Avenue (at 73rd Street)
212-717-5252

$ $ $

👙 👙 👙 👙 👙

🍴 🍴 🍴 🍴

🪑 🪑 🪑

🏠 🏠 🏠 🏠 🏠

This review covers only half of Payard. The elegant Belle Epoque pastry shop in front is a treat; the restaurant in back, which is noisy and unfriendly, is not. But it's worth a pilgrimage here just to experience the patisserie's exquisite desserts (the owner here was pastry chef at uber-restaurant Daniel, so his pedigree is excellent). If you snag one of the teeny tables, order an espresso and try to choose from one of the whimsical, sweet masterpieces: thick mousses decorated with icing images of the New York skyline, sponge cake smothered in fruit, and simple but luscious cookies, macaroons, and cakes. A must for solo-dining chocoholics.

Penang
1596 Second Avenue (at 83rd Street)
212-585-3838
See page 50.

Pizzeria Uno Chicago
220 East 86th Street (between Second and Third Avenues)
212-472-5656
See page 18.

Sarabeth's
Hotel Wales
1295 Madison Avenue (between 92nd and 93rd Streets)
212-410-7335

Whitney Museum
945 Madison Avenue (at 75th Street)
212-570-3670

$ $ / / / /
&#xfant; &#xfant;   Y Y
&#x1; &#x1; &#x1; &#x1; &#x1;   m m m

Sarabeth's is the little brunch/bake shop that grew. At heart, however, it's more a boulangerie with a few tables than it is a New York mini-chain. Sarabeth Levine—yes, there is a Sarabeth—is a James Beard "Best Pastry Chef" winner, something fans of her homemade muffins and marmalades would certainly agree with. The Solo Diner always spots fellow travelers in all of Sarabeth's places, and they always seem to be smiling. Lunch and dinner items can be inconsistent, but the seasonal chicken potpie is a favorite. Long lines for brunch, especially at her home base on the Upper West Side; lighting is excellent at each location.

Sette Mezzo
969 Lexington Avenue (between 70th and 71st Streets)
212-472-0400

$ $ $ / / / /
&#xfant; &#xfant;   Y Y
&#x1; &#x1;   m m m

The good news is that Sette Mezzo is single diner friendly. The bad news is that it's single diner friendly if you're a local regular or someone rich and famous. The restaurant functions as something of a private club for the neighborhood and is more likely to give a newcomer attitude than a table. Not that it matters, but the Northern Italian food is quite good. Feeling lucky? Cash only.

Sharz Café & Wine Bar
177 East 90th Street (between Lexington and Third)
212-874-8500

$ $

The last place The Solo Diner ever expected to find a friendly, unpretentious, reasonably priced place to relax with clean, straightforward food is the far Upper East Side. But New York is all about discoveries, and Sharz proves to be one of the best-kept secrets in an iffy neighborhood. Don't be put off by its minuscule size or the preponderance of regulars; on each visit, The Solo Diner has been warmly welcomed, and on most visits seen other solo diners at the dozen or so tables. Among the highlights from the daily blackboard menu: beefy, ruby tuna steak; perfectly cooked pasta; homey appetizers like a puree of asparagus soup; and lovely desserts. A fine selection of wines by the glass enhance the pleasure of dining here.

Sotto Cinque
1644 Second Avenue (between 85th and 86th Streets)
212-472-5563
See page 86.

Vespa Cibabuono
1625 Second Avenue (between 84th and 85th Streets)
212-472-2050

$ $

The Solo Diner took it as a good sign that upon leaving Vespa, he saw the dapper host/owner sipping an espresso, reading *Corriere Della Sera*. It's that kind of place, a rarity up here, where solo diners can let go, settle in, and feel at home. Vespa does fill up with couples and groups, but rarely to capacity, and The Solo Diner has never been treated less than graciously. Try to get one of the small tables lining the movie-poster-covered wall, or snare a table in the garden if weather permits. The food's fresh and well-prepared, if unimaginative; just-right pastas share the menu with daily fish specials and stalwarts like osso buco and calves' liver. Small but high-quality selection of wines by the glass. Lighting is adequate inside, fine in the garden.

Viand

673 Madison Avenue (between 61st and 62nd Streets)
212-751-6622

1011 Madison Avenue (at 78th Street)
212-249-8250

300 East 86th Street (at Second Avenue)
212-879-9425

$

The Solo Diner decided not to include coffee shops and diners in this book, but he's making an exception for Viand for several reasons. First, places like this are an endangered species; their survival on Madison Avenue is almost a miracle. Second, they capture something quintessentially Upper East Side that seems to be disappearing—a sort of shabby gentility that once defined this area. And third, all three locations are perfect places for solo diners to plop themselves down and relax after a hard day of window-shopping or museum-hopping. The counters are especially fun, with chatty cooks and servers. Food is much better than average; huge turkey sandwiches are a signature here, and burgers are always a good bet. Viand is also a great breakfast spot if you wake up around here. Prices are slightly higher than other diners, but worth it. Lighting is good around the clock. Wine is passable, but about what you'd expect from a coffee shop.

60TH STREET TO 96TH STREET
The Upper West Side

BEFORE GENTRIFICATION SET in ten or fifteen years ago, the Upper West Side was made up of neighbors and neighborhoods. Newcomers were either students at Columbia or Julliard, musicians, or people who felt they had become too respectable for Greenwich Village but were not yet respectable enough for the Upper East Side.

Longtime local Cuban-Chinese places abut nouvelle cuisine establishments. "Single" here is as likely to mean the retired and friendly as it does the young and frisky. And you'll see more children here than you'll see in any other part of town. If you're not wild about the stroller and cell phone set, then you'd better feed in the Lincoln Center area.

While the neighbors are gone, the sense of neighborhood lingers in most of the restaurants. Few look down on singles, especially locals. And if there were to be a reward for the area with the most establishments that have enough light to read by, it would be the Upper West Side.

Ayurveda Café

706 Amsterdam Avenue (at 94th Street)

212-932-2400

$

This tiny Indian-vegetarian bills itself as "a place for balance"; chalk one up for truth in advertising. There's a soothing little fountain inside, the ceiling is painted with clouds, and the cheap fixed-price lunch and dinner menus include appetizers, vegetable entrées, salad, rice, delicious bread, chutney, and dessert. According to the owners, the menu reflects the six essential tastes of Ayurveda (the ancient holistic system of well-being): salty, sweet, sour, bitter, astringent, and pungent. Lighting's always terrific, and the service is as well; the waiters and waitresses here always make The Solo Diner feel like a guest, not a customer. Favorite dishes include chickpeas in tomato sauce, exquisite basmati rice, and hearty but light spinach with mushrooms. If the decor here seems dull at first glance, take a minute to contemplate it; the colors (orange, pastels) are intended to promote feelings of well-being. P.S. From four to 5:30 P.M. every day this place becomes a salon of sorts, serving tea and offering impromptu readings of poetry and literature.

Barney Greengrass (The Sturgeon King)

541 Amsterdam Avenue (between 86th and 87th Streets)

212-724-4707

$ $

Barney Greengrass has been serving what many consider the city's best lox and sturgeon, along with other traditional Jewish deli favorites, since 1908. Some people who lined up back then are probably still waiting to get in. Seriously, long lines are the biggest drawback here; waits can average up to two hours on weekends. But you have to experience it at least once; dine strategically and avoid peak brunch hours and weekends. The Solo Diner's been surprised how matter-of-fact Barney Greengrass has always been about his requests for a table for one; he's treated no different than big parties, which is the best you can hope for in a place like this. Inside, you'll find brisk, efficient service; atmosphere you can cut with a knife; decor that hasn't been updated since the Taft administration, including vinyl chairs and lots of Formica; and food that will take you to heaven and back. Plates of exquisite fish, scrambled eggs and lox, chopped liver, borscht, and knishes are all textbook-perfect. Lighting is very good. No alcohol served. P.S. They close very early and don't take credit cards.

Bruculino

225 Columbus Avenue (between 70th and 71st Streets)
212-579-3966

$ $

The Solo Diner almost wrote this place off on his first visit; the prim hostess gave him a reception chillier than a New York winter. But as the evening wore on, Bruculino warmed up. The servers, without exception, were friendly and eager to please. The traditional, no-surprises Italian cooking turned out to be the perfect antidote for the frigid weather.

And the rather dimly lit room—tables covered in brown
paper, sparsely decorated walls, warm atmosphere—made
for a very enjoyable evening of solo dining. The cooking
has held up on repeat visits too. The Solo Diner can see
why celeb solo diner Jeff Simmons made this one of his
choices. Pasta fagioli, the traditional bean and pasta soup,
was dense and rich. Orange, fennel, and onion salad was
clean and invigorating. Sea bass and snapper came perfectly prepared, though a fish casserole in "a light seasoned
broth" somehow needed to be lighter and more seasoned.
Pastas arrived al dente, which is how The Solo Diner likes
them. Desserts taste store-bought, so save the splurge for a
neighborhood café. Average-quality wine list offers a fair
selection by the glass.

City Chow Cafe (at Equinox Fitness Club)
Broadway at 92nd Street
212-799-1818

Amsterdam Avenue at 76th Street
212-721-4200
See page 71.

Columbus Bakery
424 Columbus Avenue (between 82nd and 83rd Streets)
212-724-6880
See page 101.

Cosi/Xando
2160 Broadway (between 76th and 77th Streets)
212-595-5616
See page 9.

Edgar's Café

255 West 84th Street (between Broadway and West End Avenue)

212-496-6126

$

The "Edgar" in question is Poe, and this atmospheric neighborhood haunt takes inspiration from him for decor (Gothic chandelier, faux-aged walls) and food ("raven" salad of spinach and goat cheese), but fortunately not ambience. The stroller set takes over on weekends, but any other time this is a terrific place to settle into a small table, order a generous salad or sandwich, and savor the quintessentially Upper West Side environment here. Service is friendly, cheerful, and accommodating. Short, not-that-interesting wine list with a few by-the-glass options.

EJ's Luncheonette

447 Amsterdam Avenue (between 81st and 82nd Streets)

212-873-3444

See page 38.

French Roast

2340 Broadway (at 85th Street)

212-799-1533

See page 40.

Good Enough To Eat

483 Amsterdam Avenue (between 83rd and 84th Streets)

212-496-0163

$ $ 🍴 🍴 🍴

🍴 🍴   Y Y

🪑 🪑 🪑   🪑 🪑 🪑

Forget weekends, when the line for brunch runs an hour
or more. Off hours midweek are best for this folksy country inn, which helps popularize the current craze for comfort food. French toast, eggs Benedict, and meat loaf are
among the comfort foods offered here. Single-friendly when
it's not swamped by Upper East Siders on a crosstown raid.
At dinner it's downright serene.

Jackson Hole Burgers

517 Columbus Avenue (at 85th Street)
212-362-5177
See page 132.

Josie's Restaurant and Juice Bar

300 Amsterdam Avenue (at 74th Street)
212-769-1212

$ $ 🍴 🍴 🍴 🍴 🍴

🍴 🍴 🍴 🍴   Y Y Y Y

🪑 🪑 🪑   🪑 🪑 🪑

Lucky for solo diners, the juice bar that helped give this
place its name also serves Josie's full menu of well-prepared,
thoughtfully executed, and conscientiously created health
food. You can survey Josie's bright, soothing peach-colored
interior from your perch there, or wait for one of the small
tables by the Amsterdam Avenue windows (The Solo
Diner's favorite seats) to open up. Either way, service here
is warm and welcoming, with patient servers who've obviously grown accustomed to explaining the nuances of a
complicated menu. If you're expecting alfalfa-and-tofu
penance food, you're in for a very pleasant surprise; health-

ful cuisine here means appetizers like roasted butternut squash and sweet potato soup with toasted pumpkin seeds, or ginger grilled calamari with pineapple–red pepper salsa, and entrées that might include perfectly cooked grilled fish, warm macadamia breast of chicken salad, or free-range Black Angus burgers for diehard carnivores. Weekend brunch is a good bet only if you can make it up here when the place opens at 11:30; unbearable waits ensue afterward. Good choice of wines by the glass, including a couple of organic options. Lighting is good daytime, adequate in the evening.

La Caridad 78
2199 Broadway (at 78th Street)
212-874-2780
$

The Solo Diner has patronized this place since college. He has had to wait in line on every visit, and he has yet to earn any acknowledgment from any of the grumpy waiters. But that's part of the charm of this bustling, only-in-New-York Chino-Latino where chow mein shares the menu with near-perfect arroz con pollo and ropa vieja. Ideal lighting for reading, plenty of other solos at all hours, and heaping plates of food for a pittance make this a top choice on the Upper West Side. The Solo Diner's preferred tables: on your right as you enter, by the window facing Broadway. P.S. Finish off with an espresso—be sure to ask for it black.

Lemongrass Grill
494 Amsterdam Avenue (at 84th Street)
212-579-0344

2534 Broadway (between 94th and 95th Streets)
212-666-0888
See page 12.

Louie's Westside Café
441 Amsterdam Avenue (at 81st Street)
212-877-1900
$

Sharp-eyed solo diners might recognize this place from the Tom Hanks–Meg Ryan schmaltzfest *You've Got Mail*. Aside from location, the filmmakers probably chose Louie's because it's a quintessential Upper West Side hangout—reasonable prices, decent comfort food, a relaxing, high-ceilinged room (seating outdoors in season), and a warm welcome. Menu's predictable, with soups, salads, pastas, grilled fish, and chicken, but that's what you're here for. Several smaller tables; good lighting. Great people-watching from the windows on Amsterdam Avenue, which may be home to the largest concentration of strollers in the known universe.

Nick & Toni's Café
100 West 67th Street (between Broadway and Columbus)
212-496-4000
$ $ $

Many neighborhood singles seem to make this restaurant in the Lincoln Center area their home away from home.

There are two schools of thought about it: one, that it's not as good as the East Hampton original; and two, that it's a great neighborhood joint. Either way, the food—mussels roasted in a wood oven, Caesar salad, roasted chicken (also from that wood oven), and other seasonal basics—is simple and good, often with a Mediterranean twist or touch. Wine is French, mostly from the less-well-known regions, with many available by the glass.

Ollie's Broadway
1991 Broadway (at 67th Street)
212-595-8181

Ollie's Noodle Shop & Grill
2315 Broadway (at 84th Street)
212-362-3111

Ollie's Uptown
2957 Broadway (at 116th Street)
212-932-3300
See Ollie's Midtown on page 109.

Penang
240 Columbus Avenue (at 71st Street)
212-769-3988
See page 50.

Pizzeria Uno Chicago
432 Columbus Avenue (between 80th and 81st Streets)
212-595-4700
See page 18.

Popover Café

551 Amsterdam Avenue (between 86th and 87th Streets)
212-595-8555

$ $ 🍴 🍴 🍴 🍴

🪑 🪑 🪑 🍷

🧍 🧍 🧍 🧍 🧍 🪑 🪑 🪑

The first thing you notice is the teddy bears. They're all
over the dining room at this longtime Upper West Side
favorite, otherwise decorated from what looks like Laura
Ashley's garage sale. You'll also notice solo diners here more
often than not; they're drawn by the relaxed atmosphere,
friendly welcome and service, and, of course, the popovers,
served here with strawberry butter. The menu also offers
straightforward soups (served with a popover), salads
(ditto), omelettes, unusual egg creations ("cappuccino eggs,"
anyone? They're whipped and steamed), and cutesy sandwiches ("The Butler Did It" features smoked salmon, cream
cheese, tomato, and watercress on pumpernickel). Lighting
is very good all day and evening. One very important
caveat: avoid this place on weekends if you value your sanity. The queues for brunch resemble some yuppie-parent
version of a Soviet bread line. A riot always seems immi-
nent. And the waits seem to grow every week.

Republic

2290 Broadway (between 82nd and 83rd Streets)
212-579-5959
See page 85.

Sarabeth's

423 Amsterdam Avenue (between 80th and 81st Streets)
212-496-6280
See page 135.

Zen Palate

2170 Broadway (between 76th and 77th Streets)
212-501-7768
See page 90.

THE TABLE FOR ONE
HALL OF FAME

As READERS could probably tell from the tone of The Solo Diner's comments, there are a number of places in New York that represent the best of everything solo diners would want at a table for one. Those establishments have been inducted into the Table for One Hall of Fame; long may they reign. In alphabetical order:

1. **Candle Café**, 1307 Third Avenue
   Blessedly attitude-free sanctuary on the attitude-heavy Upper East Side.

2. **Chez Brigitte**, 77 Greenwich Avenue
   Brigitte, whoever she is, should be patron saint of solo dining; this tiny West Village counter practically invented it.

3. **Eisenberg Sandwich Shop**, 174 Fifth Avenue
   Where Edward Hopper might hang out in 2001 New York; an authentic holdout in the super-trendified Flatiron district.

4. **Florent**, 69 Gansevoort Street
   Which is cooler, the counter or the tables? Trick
   question. The whole place is cool.

5. **Gotham Bar & Grill**, 123 East 12th Street
   Solo-diner heaven looks a lot like the bar here.

6. **La Caridad 78**, 2199 Broadway
   The Solo Diner would pay just to sit at the window
   tables and watch Upper Broadway go by.

7. **Mayrose**, 920 Broadway
   Lots of small tables, cool music, and a massive basket of newspapers on the happening counter—what
   more do you want?

8. **New Pasteur Restaurant**, 85 Baxter Street
   No matter how packed, they always seem to have
   room for solo diners.

9. **Peacock Alley**, 301 Park Avenue
   Worth every dollar; The Solo Diner's favorite
   splurge.

10. **Thali**, 28 Greenwich Avenue
    You'll walk out floating from this tiny West Village
    Indian.

The Table for One
Hall of Shame

Finally, the solo diner is thrilled to present the Table for One Hall of Shame—ten establishments that do their best to turn your solo-dining experience into an extended episode of psychological warfare. The Solo Diner has suffered so you don't have to. Drumroll, please:

1. **"44,"** Hotel Royalton, 44 West 44th Street
   Hotel restaurant that makes you feel like a guest who's overstayed your welcome.

2. **The Viceroy**, 160 Eighth Avenue
   Without a muscle-bound Chelsea boy at your side, forget getting attention from anyone, especially the waiters.

3. **E.A.T.**, 1064 Madison Avenue
   If you want to pay huge sums of money to be ignored, this is your place.

4. **Life Café**, 343 East 10th Street
   Made famous by Rent. Maybe The Solo Diner's not "downtown" enough; they couldn't be bothered serving him on several occasions.

5. **Le Madri**, 168 West 18th Street
   There's a gulag in the rear where solo diners are welcome.

6. **Coffee Shop**, 29 Union Square West
   You want what? Food? I'm busy.

7. **Casa La Femme**, 150 Wooster Street
   You've seen the classic film *Contempt*. Now experience the restaurant.

8. **Ernie's**, 2150 Broadway
   So big the servers need rollerblades. Too bad they whiz right by solo diners.

9. **Coco Pazzo Teatro**, 235 West 46th Street
   Overdone, overbooked, overburdened.

10. **Rachel's American Bistro**, 608 Ninth Avenue
    The maitre d' actually yelled at The Solo Diner for draping his coat on another table's chair—even though the dining room was empty.

INDEX